JADE OF THE EAST

JADE
OF THE EAST

BY GEOFFREY WILLS

New York WEATHERHILL Tokyo

A NOTE ON DECORATIONS. The title-page photograph is a detail of the incense burner shown in Plate 122. The binding design is based upon a small brown-jade pendant from an ancient Chinese tomb (collection of M. Weatherby).

First edition, 1972
Second printing, 1977

Published by John Weatherhill, Inc., of New York and Tokyo, with editorial offices at 7-6-13 Roppongi, Minato-ku, Tokyo 106, Japan. Copyright © 1972 by Geoffrey Wills; all rights reserved. Printed in Japan.

LCC Card No. 72-78589   ISBN 0-8348-1854-x

TABLE OF CONTENTS

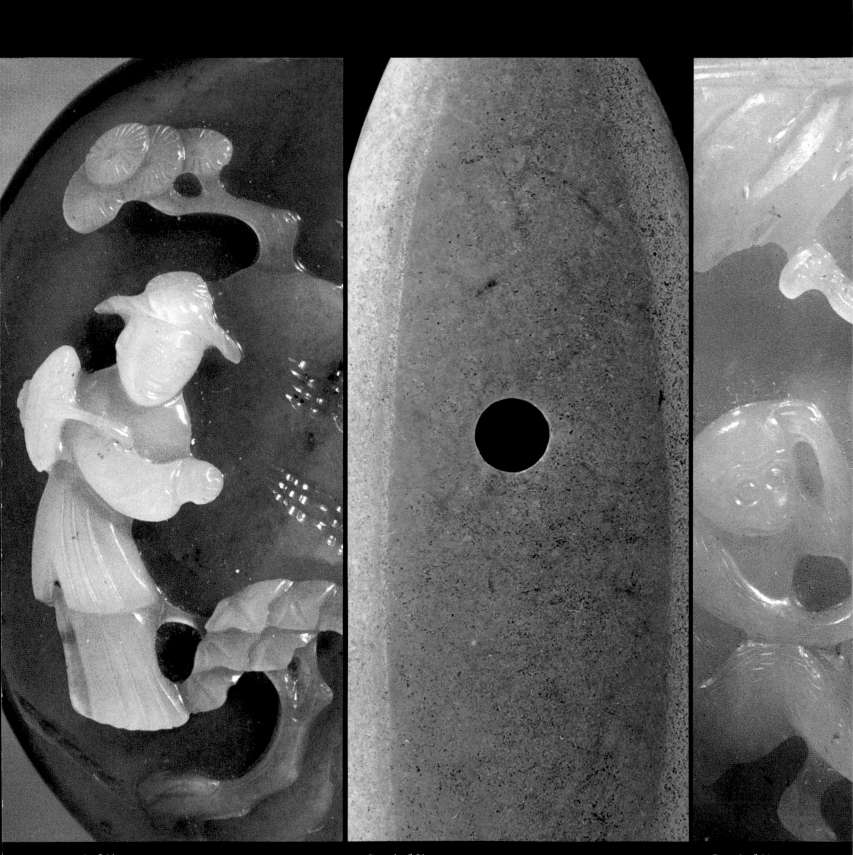

1. *Detail of Plate 90.* 2. *Detail of Plate 149.* 3. *Detail of Plate 89.*

4. *Detail of Plate 92.*

5. *Detail of Plate 126.*

LIST OF ILLUSTRATIONS

PREFACE

IN THIS book I have attempted to write a balanced account of the jade found in Asia and New Zealand and the forms into which it has been worked.

Jade has managed to retain, right into the twentieth century, a high proportion of the mystery attached to it over a period of thousands of years. In the case of China, the stone epitomizes the country's culture, and despite the considerable advances that have been made in unraveling many of the complex problems related to it, there are still many others that defy elucidation.

As much as any other author of a factual work, I am greatly indebted to those who have preceded me in the field. In particular, I acknowledge my obligation to the books of Professor S. Howard Hansford, and am grateful to the owners and guardians of the jades illustrated for their kindness in allowing the use of photographs. Finally, I thank Dr. F. A. Turk for his generous and helpful counsel.

G. W.

PART ONE

CHINESE JADE

CHAPTER ONE

ORIGINS OF CHINESE JADE

IN THE Western mind the word jade almost automatically conjures up the word China, together with the entire civilisation of that land and its people. The Chinese, too, have always regarded jade as a substance peculiarly Chinese, and symbolic of their long heritage.

Jade is a stone varying in colour and translucence, but the name is applied indiscriminately to what are in reality two distinct types of mineral: nephrite and jadeite. The difference between them is generally apparent to the eye, but sometimes it is important to make a positive identification, and to do this a knowledge of their physical properties and chemistry is necessary.

Nephrite is a variety of amphibole varying in colour according to the amount of ferrous oxide with which it has been contaminated. In its pure form it is white, and the presence of iron results in a wide range of greens, light and dark in shade according to the quantity of impurity present. Structurally nephrite is composed of matted fibrous crystals resembling asbestos, and some asbestos is, in fact, a form of amphibole. Nephrite is roughly of the same hardness as glass, and on the scale of testing known by the name of the mineralogist Friedrich Mohs, it is listed at $5\frac{1}{2}$ to $6\frac{1}{2}$. Its specific gravity ranges between 2.90 and 3.02.

SCALE OF HARDNESS
(Devised in 1820 by Friedrich Mohs)

1	Talc	6	Feldspar
2	Gypsum	7	Quartz
3	Calcite	8	Topaz
4	Fluor	9	Corundum
5	Apatite	10	Diamond

Jadeite, on the other hand, is of crystalline formation and is a variety of pyroxene, which is itself related to the amphiboles. It is found in a much wider colour range than nephrite, and is noteworthy for the occurrence of a brilliant emerald green. This colour is due to the presence of the metallic element chromium, and is mostly found in the form of streaks across a whitish ground, or is seen in mottled light and dark tints. Jadeite also occurs in shades of mauve, yellow, blue, brown, and red as well as in grey and white. Some of these colours also appear in nephrite, so colour alone cannot be taken as a certain indication of jadeite.

Jadeite has a hardness of $6\frac{1}{2}$ to 7, equal to that of quartz on the Mohs scale, and its specific gravity varies between 3.30 and 3.36: in both instances giving a higher reading than nephrite. Apart from its sometimes unique colours which, as mentioned above, are not in themselves always conclusive, jadeite differs in its polished state from its brother stone. Nephrite takes on what has been aptly termed "a greasy lustre," while jadeite can be given a bright, glasslike shine. The surface of the latter is often seen to be uneven or dimpled, due to small spots of slightly softer material having been rubbed down below the principal hard areas.

A further difference between the two varieties of jade is not normally visible to the eye and only becomes apparent as a result of drastic testing or by accident. Heating to about 1025° Centigrade results in jadeite being reduced to a glassy mass, while nephrite becomes whitish in colour and opaque.[1] Nephrite, on the contrary, does not change in shape and carving in it remains unaltered, but the surface sometimes develops a fine network of cracks and the stone may lose some of its hardness in the heating process.

The tint acquired by burnt nephrite is also present on a high proportion of pieces that have been excavated after prolonged burial. It is known to the Chinese as *chi ku pi,* "chicken-bone white," and is much esteemed in that country. The fact that a sign of age can be counterfeited in this way must be borne in mind when deciding on the authenticity of specimens.

The high regard in which jade was held, was due to its rarity and to the extreme difficulty of working such a hard stone. At one time jade was found only in small quantities, and in so few and such remote places, that when pieces of it eventually reached the carver's bench they had travelled far and were consequently very costly.

The oldest known of the two stones is nephrite, of which simply carved pieces dating from Neolithic times are on record. They were the work of Chinese craftsmen, and with inadequate research bolstered by national pride, successive writers in China have alleged that the basic material originally came from their own soil. Modern study has been quite unable to discover proof for such statements, and it is widely accepted that they are erroneous. Continued confusion has been caused by the fact that the Chinese persistently employed the term *yü* to describe not only jade, but other stones as well. These include, on occasion, various kinds of minerals and marble,[2] so that references to *yü* in ancient writings are of debatable significance when seeking reliable records of jade.

In 1736 one writer recorded that supplies of the stone came from Suchou, in the province of Kansu, and the presence of nephrite there was apparently confirmed by a visiting mineralogist in 1890. As recently as 1913, this material was finally proved to be serpentine, which is a rock of very different composition. Other areas that have enjoyed a temporary interest for the same reason include Anyang, the province of Yünnan, and Lan-t'ien. The last, which lies in Shensi Province, was recorded as a source of jade in an encyclopaedia completed in A.D. 983, as well as in a medical work of 1596. A later writer has suggested that the Lan-t'ien referred to in these works was not the one in Shensi, but another situated in the mountains of Khotan.[3]

Khotan is the name of a town, and of the oasis in which it is situated, bounded on three sides by desert and on the fourth by the K'unlun mountains. The town stands on what was one of the most important Asian trading routes, and after being conquered by the Chinese in A.D. 73, its stability was assured and its prosperity increased. Following its capture in the eighth century by an Arab chieftain, Kotaiba ibn Moslim, who came from West Turkestan, the place was destroyed in 1220 by Genghis Khan.

It seems that Khotan was quickly reconstructed, for in 1274, when the Venetian traveller Marco Polo was there, the town was again a flourishing place. He noted that, "Everything is to be had there in plenty, including abundance of cotton, with flax, hemp, wheat, wine and the like. The people have vineyards and gardens and estates. They live by commerce and manufactures, and are no soldiers." It may be added that while both grapes and wine were praised highly by tenth-century Chinese writers, a more modern author agreed as regards the grapes but said the wine was "detestable."

Some centuries after Marco Polo's visit, in the 1750s, Khotan and the country thereabouts was again the scene of warfare, and after some years of fighting came under Chinese rule. A hundred years later, a revolt took place and was followed by the capture of the country by Yakub Beg of Kashgar. He, in his turn, suffered defeat, and the area then became a province of China.

It was, in fact, from Khotan in Chinese Turkestan that supplies of nephrite were obtained over a period of two thousand years or more. References to the place of origin can be found in literary works datable to the second century B.C. when Huai-nan Tzu, a philosopher of the Han dynasty, wrote about a stone from Khotan that withstood three days and nights of heating in a furnace. Allowing for some exaggeration, and the lack of any indication about the degree of temperature reached by the furnace, this stone would appear to have been nephrite. From that date onward, there are numerous and less controversial references to the finding of the stone in that area.

The Khotan oasis is watered by two rivers, the Kara-kāsh (Black Jade River) and the Yurung-kāsh (White Jade River), which unite at a point some 145 kilometres to the north of the city and flow on across the Taklamakan desert with a fall of 380 metres over a distance of 435 kilometres. The twin rivers irrigate the oasis, and their beds were the source of some of the nephrite. Other supplies of the stone came from the mountains, whence the water flows, and naturally enough the town of Khotan was a centre for Chinese merchants who came to buy it.

Khotan's role as a source of nephrite began to be usurped in the seventeenth

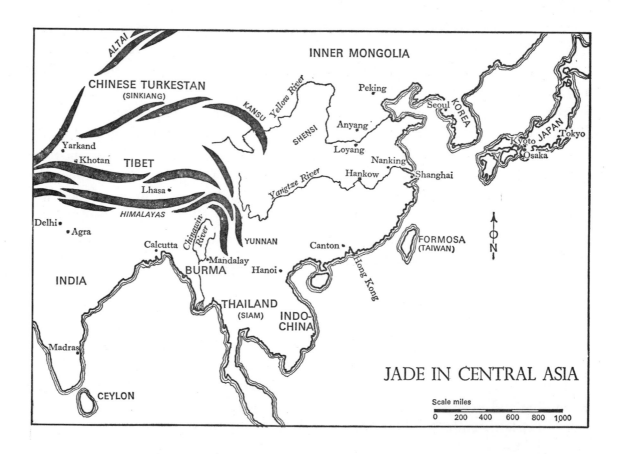

JADE IN CENTRAL ASIA

century by Yarkand, 320 kilometres or so to the northwest. Both towns lay to the north of the same long range of great mountains, from which the river Zaraf-shān descended to Yarkand. In a history of Chinese Turkestan (*Hsi yü wên chien lu*), written in 1778 by a Manchu named Ch'i-shi-i, there is a glowing description of what lay in the territory: "There is a river in Yarkand in which are found Jade pebbles. The largest are as big as round fruit dishes, or square peck measures, the smallest are the size of a fist or chestnut, and some of the boulders weigh more than five hundred pounds. There are many different colours, among which snow white, kingfisher green, beeswax yellow, cinnabar red, and ink black are all considered valuable; but the most difficult to find are pieces of pure mutton fat texture with vermillion spots, and others of bright spinach green flecked with shining points of gold, so that these two varieties rank as the rarest and most precious of jades."

A Chinese writer has conveniently divided nephrite into categories according to the predominant colour, but without reference to rarity:

1. *Fen,* "clear water colour," perhaps an alternate phrase for "indeterminate"
2. *Pi,* indigo blue
3. *Pi,* (Pronounced in the same way as the foregoing but written differently in Chinese), moss green
4. *Kau,* yellow
5. *Fu,* the colour of a kingfisher's feathers
6. *Chiung,* cinnabar red
7. *Mên,* blood red
8. *Haieh,* lacquer black
9. *Cha,* opaque white, familiar in the West as "mutton fat"

Marco Polo noted that the inhabitants of the area obtained what he called "chalcedonies and jaspers" from the rivers, but a later European visitor, Benedict Goës, was slightly more informative. He recorded in 1603 that the stone from the rivers was esteemed above that quarried in the mountains. It was sought, he wrote, "almost in the same way in which divers fish for gems, and this is usually extracted in pieces about as big as large flints."

A Chinese writer of 1637, Sung Ying-hsing, stated that the jade searchers were often active in the autumn, and chose moonlit nights for their task because the stone had the quality of reflecting such light. In spite of this alleged natural fluorescence, the haul would be a mixed one and had to be carefully sorted. The same writer mentioned that *yü* was considered to be masculine in character, so it followed naturally that women seekers would be attracted to it, and vice versa. A woodcut in his book depicts three determined naked ladies busy in the flowing waters of the Kara-kāsh. However, the writer airily excused himself from sharing the belief by adding, "This is perhaps foolishness on the part of the natives."

The stones and boulders washed down from the heights and lying in the rivers were the first sources of jade to be exploited, and it was not until the twelfth century A.D. that quarrying received a mention. It was carried out, according to

1. *Naked women and girls collecting pebbles of jade from a river. From* T'ien Kung K'ai Wu *by Sung Ying-hsing.*

Goës, at a remote spot which lay some twenty days' travel from Yarkand—possibly the same place mentioned a century later as being situated 230 li from the city. Sung Ying-hsing, whose descriptions of the arts and industries of his country include many facts mixed with a percentage of improbabilities, stated that prior to quarrying the jade was as soft as cotton wool.

Tales of this kind are not uncommon throughout old literature wherever there are mentions of the stone. They are understandable in view of the inaccessibility of sources of the material, which would force most writers to rely on hearsay, or copy from their predecessors. Moreover, merchants and others concerned in obtaining and marketing the stone would be eager to safeguard their livelihood from possible rivals, and at the same time ensure that jade kept a high and steady value, by encouraging the spread of such legends.

Of the actual quarrying, little is recorded, but a mention is made by Benedict Goës of the fact that fire played a part. In his own words, fire was employed "to soften the stone," but this is most probably a misunderstanding on his part, or on someone else's, of its use for the purpose. His phrase implies that the jade was melted to free it from its surrounding of worthless stone and, presumably, it quickly reset to its normal hardness. In fact, heat was applied to split it away from its bed and to break it into masses of the size required.

This rough-and-ready method was not only immensely wasteful, but in addition to the stone that was broken through mischance, a proportion of the usable pieces suffered internal damage. Such fractures would rarely be visible to the eye until the jade reached the lapidary and he began to remove the parts surplus to his requirements. Thus, there was a strong predilection for river jade, which had suffered only the buffetings of nature and none from the clumsy hand of man.

The smooth stones brought up from the rivers had acquired with time, through contact with the air, water, and earth, an outer "skin" of brown colour. This effectively disguised the beauty that lay within, but many of the carvers saw the skin as giving an additional charm to their finished work. They planned their carvings in such a way as to include in the design a portion of the brown material, which appeared in pleasing contrast to the tint of the jade itself.

Turning to the other form of the stone, jadeite, the story is quite different. Jadeite has a considerably shorter history than nephrite, but exactly how and when it came into use has not been discovered. At present there is no evidence that it was known or used in China prior to the mid-eighteenth century, and objects carved from it must therefore have been made after that time.

The stone was found in the treacherous country of the far north of Burma, to the west of Myitkyina and north of Mogaung. There, the fast-flowing Uru (or Uyu) river, a tributary of the Irrawaddy, has cut its way through the land in places to make gorges flanked by steep cliffs. Both the Uru and streams flowing into it brought down boulders as they descended from the mountains where they rose, and over the centuries a mass of stone and earth was deposited—the so-called Uru Boulder Conglomerate, which ranges in width from two to four miles, partly forming the beds of the river and streams and their banks. A traveller who saw the jade workings in 1837 wrote: "The stone is found in the form of more or less rounded boulders mixed with other boulders of various rocks . . . embedded in a brick-coloured yellow, or nearly orange-coloured clay, which forms the soil of the valley, and which is of considerable depth."[4]

Nearly a century later, an Indian geologist, H. L. Chhibber, recorded what was then taking place, methods that would appear to have changed little or not at all from those of the past: "Generally, at the top is some overburden (alluvium), which is sluiced away by a water-race formed by diverting the channel of a stream. Then the Boulder Conglomerate is quarried with picks, crowbars and *mamooties,* so that a steep face is obtained. Water dammed a little upstream is made to flow as a race over this steep face, which washing away all the earth, leaves the boulders clearly exposed to view. They are carefully examined for jadeite."[5]

Chhibber added that, even in 1928, "the work is not all carried out on up-to-date scientific lines, but in the old primitive fashion. The people work blindly believing entirely in their luck." As late as 1888 they burned bamboo, watching the behaviour of the sticks, flames, and smoke so as to decide what action they should take. On finding a vein of the stone, further divination was resorted to, in order to discover if the material should be worked at once or left, in the belief that the colour would mature.

As in the case of nephrite, the truth about jadeite is often found interlarded with legend. The most persistent legend is the statement that the stone was imported into China from the thirteenth century onwards. Not only is there no mention of a Burmese origin in Oriental literature until five hundred years later, but no specimens of jadeite older than the eighteenth century have been recorded.

The source of the stories is a Mr. Warry of the Chinese Consular Service, whose report on what he saw in 1888 was published some years later.[6] He wrote: "The discovery that green jade of fine quality occurred in Northern Burma was made accidentally by a small Yünnanese trader in the 13th century. The story runs that on returning from a journey across the frontier he picked up a piece of stone to balance the load on his mule. The stone proved to be jade of great value and a large party went back to procure more of it. In this errand they were unsuccessful, nobody being able to inform them where the stone occurred. Another attempt, equally fruitless, was made by the Yünnan Government in the fourteenth century to discover the stone; all the members of the expedition, it is said, perished by malaria, or at the hands of hostile hill-tribes." He added that from then onwards, for several centuries, there was no similar activity, but after 1784 hostilities between China and Burma terminated "and from this time dates the opening of a regular trade between the two countries."

Warry stated that local conditions made the collection of jade extremely hazardous. A difficult terrain with a malarial climate was inhabited by warlike tribes, so that no more than a score or so of Chinese went there each year, "and a very small proportion of these ever returned." He continued: "In the Chinese temple at Amarapura is a long list containing the names of upwards of 6,000 Chinese traders deceased in Burma since the beginning of the present [nineteenth] century to whom funeral rites are yearly paid. The large majority of these men are known to have lost their lives in the search for jade. The roll includes only the names of well-known and substantial traders. Could the number of small traders and adventurers who perished in the same enterprise be ascertained, the list would be swelled to many times its size."

The range of colours in which jadeite has been found was mentioned earlier (page 15). Of them all, the most esteemed and usually the most costly, is the bright emerald green. Because its distinctive colour may be compared with that of the bird's plumage, green jadeite is known in China by the name of a kingfisher found there: fei-ts'ui. Within recent decades, use of the term has spread to the West, and especially in the United States it is not uncommon to read of a piece described simply as "fei-ts'ui jade."

The attractive feathers of the kingfisher were used for decorative purposes by the Chinese from early times, and a fourth century B.C. poem mentions "coverlets of fei-ts'ui and pearls."[7] The term fei-ts'ui was occasionally applied during the Sung dynasty to a dark green nephrite, but was revived in the eighteenth century for the jadeite. The reuse of the neglected term, although applied to a material totally different in colour and composition, might account for the erroneous notion that jadeite had been known in the distant past.

As with nephrite, the stone can be listed according to its colour and marking, and Chhibber noted in 1927 that the Burmese merchants then divided it into eight categories. They were as follows:[8]

1. *Mya yay* or *yay kyauk,* the most precious, of a translucent grass green colour
2. *Shwelu,* light green with bright green markings
3. *Lat yay,* clouded
4. *Hmaw sit sit,* dark green, "rather soft and brittle"
5. *Konpi,* red or brownish, found in boulders which have been embedded in red earth
6. *Kyauk-atha,* translucent white
7. *Pan-tha,* white and translucent, but sometimes with opaque patches which reduce its value
8. *Kyauk ame,* dark green, which appears black unless the material is cut thinly

It is interesting and perhaps surprising that neither blue nor mauve colours are included in this list. The red or brownish variety called *konpi* acquires its colour from the earth in which it has long been embedded, and the colour is due to "the dissemination of ferruginous matter by percolating water." Chhibber says that the stain penetrates no more than one-third of an inch into the interior. Like the very similar dark brown found on the outer layers of nephrite boulders, this stained portion was sometimes subtly used by the jade carvers.

Whether nephrite or jadeite, the precious material had to be brought to some convenient market centre before it could be sold and forwarded to China. Most of the stone went overland by lengthy and often labyrinthine routes to China but some, after journeying on the backs of coolies or in bullock carts through the Burmese country, or even making its way down the Irrawaddy river on bamboo rafts, arrived at Rangoon for shipment to the China ports. No matter which route was taken, the journey of jade to its destination in the hands of the Chinese carver was a long and perilous one involving considerable labour and risk.

The Chinese craftsman duly chose the piece that seemed to suit his requirements. In so doing he had to exercise considerable powers of judgement, for, unlike the sculptor who can select from a variety of stones some piece from which he can carve a preconceived form, the jade carver's idea of what he will carve is largely dictated by the piece of jade itself. He has to visualise a finished object within a rounded or shapeless lump that might later reveal hitherto concealed flaws that will further modify the form of the completed work. Moreover, a piece of jade is worth considerably more than a piece of marble or other stone of comparable size. Wastage is very costly, and the greatest possible use has to be made of the material.

The carver relies on his experienced eye to estimate the potential of the material before him, trusting that natural colour-faults and man-made fractures within will not impair or ruin the result. A river boulder with its red or brown "skin" poses a further problem: a decision must be made about whether all or part of the outer surface is to be retained, or whether it should be discarded completely. This problem is resolved in part by the carver's own taste, in part by the object itself, which may or may not be suitable for displaying such contrasting colours, and in part by the taste of prospective buyers under the influence of prevailing fashion.

In modern times a considerable amount of argument has taken place on the subject of jade working in the past. References to the actual carving process are very few in ancient literature, possibly due to ignorance on the part of the writers caused by the secrecy of carvers, and partly, no doubt, due to the general indifference to technical matters shown by Chinese writers. This lack of information has led to the publication of what are simply wild guesses, perhaps sincerely held even if untenable, that have had to be demolished. Of these guesses, the most odd and persistent concerns the "*k'un-wu* knife," which was alleged to cut jade "as if it were clay." A reference to this marvelous instrument appeared as early as the fourth century B.C., to be followed by a further mention of it a century later, and repetitions in more modern times.

In his book *The Diamond,* published in 1915, the sinologist Berthold Laufer mistranslated passages from ancient Chinese authors in order to demonstrate that the precious stone had been employed for jade carving in early times. He was thus able to prove to his own satisfaction the correctness of his theory that a "*k'un-wu* knife" was none other than a diamond. In one particular instance he rendered a sentence in the *The Official History of the Sung Dynasty* as: "The substance nephrite is hard, but not quite so hard as a diamond-point." Professor Hansford states that the words should read: "Jade is an extremely hard material, and can only be carved by means of the *k'un-wu* knife and toad-grease."

A commonsense view is that the statement about using a knife to cut jade was no more than a turn of speech. It was a commendation of the quality of the metal, applied to it in much the same manner as that in which a hero is referred to as being "as strong as a lion." This does not imply that the man of courage resembles a lion in appearance or, for that matter, roars instead of speaking normally.

The curious term toad grease recalls a further source of long-lasting dispute. This evil-sounding substance was supposed to possess the power of softening nephrite to the consistency of wax or clay, so that it could be shaped and carved without difficulty. In this instance the term has been taken literally by subsequent writers, and a Chinese author of A.D. 500 solemnly advised his readers who were unable to obtain the genuine article that chopped fat meat, fried, was equally effective. According to him, "This also makes it [jade] soft and slippery, so that it may be easily carved."

It is, of course, quite impossible that a grease, or any other unguent or liquid, could act in the way attributed to toad grease. Reports of it and its almost magical action may have been due to complete ignorance on the part of successive writers; the earliest of them not properly understanding his subject, and the others blindly following his lead. In recent times it has been realised that the term "toad grease" is applied in China to many kinds of grease from different sources. We have a modern parallel, in the use of so-called bear's grease in the name of a Victorian and Edwardian pomade that did not necessarily originate in that animal.

It is likely, however, that grease was used together with an abrasive powder, so as to keep the latter where it was wanted. Without something of the kind the powder would have to be continually applied, involving a waste of time, labour, and material. Nowadays, carborundum powder is sold ready-mixed in the form of a paste for use in grinding engine valves, and toad grease may well have been a similar composition. Perhaps, also, modern translators should have made allowances for an ancient Chinese sense of humour.

At various periods jade has been cut by the use of abrasives applied to it in different ways. At first, the cutting powder was rubbed painstakingly against the jade, using pieces of bamboo or anything else at hand that was considered suitable. Then, with the advent of the Bronze Age, metal became available and more precise results could be obtained than were formerly possible. Thin slices of the stone might then be cut with the aid of a wire, or even a saw, in conjunction with an abrasive.

There followed a few changes in detail, such as the introduction of improved abrasives, but the craft changed little until modern times. Evidence of how jade was worked can be seen in finished specimens, which show an increasing precision of craftsmanship as the centuries advance. Written descriptions are almost nonexistent, and it was apparently not until the seventeenth century that there appeared a reference to the use of rotary wheels for grinding the stone. Even as late in date as that, an author referred to the belief that fine carving was executed by cutting the softened material with a special knife.

While it is accepted that the shaping of jade is called "carving," the word is no more than a compromise because of the lack of any more suitable term in the English language. Carving implies slicing or chipping in the same way as is done with marble or wood or ivory, but jade is too hard and close textured for such treatment. The stone can be shaped only by cutting it to a rough form, and then laboriously grinding away the surplus. Even with the use of modern tools this is a lengthy process, and in the past it must inevitably have been more difficult and even more time-consuming.

Once the general form of the future piece had been achieved by sawing away the major surplus of stone, the next step was to make the cavities required in the final design. A bowl or a vase had to be hollowed out, for example, and its handles pierced. For these tasks a bamboo or metal tube would be used in rotary fashion to make a circular cut of the correct depth. The resulting "plug" would then be carefully tapped until it separated. A dish would be given its concavity by a series of crisscross sawcuts, thus reducing the waste material to a number of small pieces that could be ground out with comparative ease.

The interlinked rings so much admired on some of the elaborate pieces of the Ch'ien-lung era were cut and sawn with incredible patience. So well are they made and finished that it is not always realised that each link was once a part of the same block of jade as its neighbour and of the vase from which all the links hang. In exceptional instances a vase has its removable cover connected to the body by a jade chain, the whole having been formed from a single piece of stone.

As work on a piece made progress and it began to approach closely the desired result, different types of abrasive were employed. As successive stages were reached the abrasive used was finer until eventually less and less of the jade was removed and a smooth polished surface was gradually produced. Every nook and cranny had to be treated in this way, until nephrite acquired its characteristic dull shine and jadeite glistened brilliantly.

There appears to be no information at present on the subject of workshop organisation in the past. We do not know if one craftsman laboured on a piece from start to finish. While it seems reasonable to expect a single craftsman in the case of early examples of simple pattern, the more complex jades of later date may well have passed through the hands of a succession of specialists.

A precedent for this was to be seen in operation at the great porcelain kilns at Ching-tê Chên, and was mentioned by the missionary Père d'Entrecolles in a letter dated September 1, 1712. "The painting of chinaware," he wrote, "is distributed in the same workshop among a great number of workmen. One workman does nothing but draw the first colour line beneath the rims of the pieces; another traces flowers, which a third one paints; this man is painting water and mountains, and that one either birds or other animals."[9] If there was division of labour in one craft, why not also in another?

While there are many gaps in present-day knowledge of the history of jade and its working, the material itself was for a long time the subject of misconceptions in the Western world. Dr. Johnson defined the stone in his *Dictionary* as "a species of the Jasper," giving currency to what was popularly thought to be a fact. A more accurate description appeared in a book published in 1735,[10] some thirty years before Johnson's magnum opus, where it was termed "a greenish stone, bordering on the colour of olive, much esteemed for its hardness, which exceeds that of porphyry, agate, and jasper, and is only to be cut with the powder of Diamond."

As late as the 1850s jade was referred to as "serpentine":[11] a mottled green stone with a hardness between 3 and 4, compared with the $6\frac{1}{2}$ of true jade. Closer in its characteristics to the latter is chloromelanite, a variety which has a good proportion of iron in its composition. It is not very attractive in appearance, as its limited range of colour varies only between dark green and black.

The introduction of jade to Europe took place in the sixteenth century, when Spanish adventurers returned from South America bringing with them stones of a type hitherto unknown. They related that the inhabitants of the continent thought highly of the green pebbles because of their alleged efficacy as amulets against certain illnesses. In particular, persons wearing one or more pieces of jade about the body might gain relief if inflicted with a disease of the kidneys. It was on this account that the material was known as *piedra de los riñones* (literally, stone of the kidneys). This last was rendered into Latin as *lapis nephriticus,* and in due time the stone became known as nephrite. Alternatively it was called *piedra de ijada* (stone of the loins), and from it the word *ijada* was rendered as "jade."

The word nephrite was at one time applied in learned circles indiscriminately to both nephrite and jadeite, and only in 1863 was it proved by the French geologist, Alexis Damour, that they were completely different from one another in composition, nephrite belonging to the amphibole family, and jadeite to the pyroxene. As a result of Damour's work it was proposed and accepted that the two names should be applied in the manner which remains current.

Although this distinction was welcome in one way, in another it introduced a formidable ambiguity. The original stone brought from South America, *lapis nephriticus,* the reliever of kidney and other ailments, was a pyroxene, whereas the sole variety used until the eighteenth century by the Chinese was an amphibole. Damour made the error of calling the true *nephriticus* pyroxene jadeite, and the Oriental variety, nephrite; thereby giving the latter an apparent connexion with a medicinal purpose it never possessed.

The contradiction, like so many others, remained largely unremarked for almost a century, but in 1961 a publication drew attention to it. In his *Jade, Fact and Fable* the late Sir Charles Hardinge, a keen collector of Oriental carvings, discussed the history of the stone, and put forward a suggestion that the names of the two kinds should be rationalised. He wrote: "I propose to use the family names [amphibole and pyroxene] of the minerals, instead of the terms nephrite and jadeite. I shall use jade only when an 'umbrella' term is required to cover both minerals."

However, in spite of the logic of the argument, too much time has passed for any such change to be successfully accomplished. Misapplied as it is admitted they are, the words nephrite and jadeite have by now been used for so long that any alteration, especially to such unfamiliar terms as amphibole and pyroxene, is most unlikely to receive any but limited recognition.

PRINCIPAL CHINESE DYNASTIES AND REIGNS

Shang		c.1520–1030 B.C.
Chou		c.1030–221 B.C.
	Early Chou	c.1030–722 B.C.
	Ch'un Ch'iu	722–480 B.C.
	Warring States	480–221 B.C.
Ch'in		221–207 B.C.
Han		202 B.C.–A.D. 220
T'ang		618–906
Sung		960–1279
Yüan		1280–1368
Ming		1368–1644
Ch'ing		1644–1911
	K'ang-hsi	1661–1722
	Yung-chêng	1723–1735
	Ch'ien-lung	1735–1796
	Chia-ch'ing	1796–1820

CHAPTER TWO

EARLY CHINESE JADE

(Through the Yüan Dynasty)

SHAPES AND SYMBOLS

IN ANY discussion of ancient jades, consideration must be given to the problems of time and place regarding both manufacture and discovery. In respect to the latter, only in recent decades have controlled excavations been carried out and the results carefully recorded by competent persons. Even so, the published reports are few in number and mostly unsatisfactory in content, so that attributions have had to be based in most instances on literary sources or on comparable artifacts in bronze and other materials whose dates are more clearly ascertainable.

Serious Western interest in jade barely antedates the twentieth century, and the historic publication on the subject commissioned by the American collector Heber R. Bishop, may be regarded as its starting point in the English tongue. Bishop commissioned a number of prominent authorities from all parts of the world to prepare two large-sized volumes called *Investigations and Studies in Jade,* which he published privately in New York in 1906. The book embodied the most up-to-date information on the subject, and only one hundred copies were printed. They were presented to reigning monarchs, heads of state, and to the principal museums and libraries of many countries, so that today the two great volumes can usually be consulted only with some difficulty. The location of the copies is in itself inconvenient, and the fact that they weigh no less than a hundred and twenty-five pounds limits their handling for any length of time to readers in the prime of health.

The work was edited by G. F. Kunz, and its most eminent contributor was the British expert S. W. Bushell, who not only dealt with Chinese jade but translated an essay on it written especially for the book by T'ang Jung-tso of Peking. The numerous illustrations include a set of twelve original paintings, each of them executed one hundred times by a Chinese artist, showing the processes of jade carving.[1] The second volume contains descriptions of the nine hundred specimens then in the Bishop Collection, of which about two hundred were presented by the owner to the Metropolitan Museum of Art, New York.

A few years later another American, Berthold Laufer, wrote an extensive work entitled *Jade, a Study in Chinese Archaeology and Religion,* published in Chicago in

1912 (reprinted, New York, 1967). In the introduction he listed the literary sources on which he and other scholars based their attributions. They were as follows:

> 1. *K'ao ku t'u*—*Investigations of Antiquities with Illustrations,* by Lü Ta-lin, in ten chapters, first published during the Sung dynasty in 1092, and re-edited by Huang Shêng in 1753 as an appendix to Wang Fu's *Po ku t'u.* In Chapter 8 a small collection of jades in the possession of Li Po-shih from Lu-kiang is figured, but without investigation.
>
> 2. *Ku yü t'u*—*Ancient Jades Illustrated* by Chu Têh-jun, in two chapters, published 1341, and republished in 1753 with the edition of the *Po ku t'u* mentioned. The explanations appended to the illustrations are meagre.
>
> 3. *Ku yü t'u p'u*—*Illustrated Description of Ancient Jades* in 100 chapters, being the collection of jade belonging to the first emperor of the Southern Sung dynasty, Kao-tsung (A.D. 1127–62) and consisting of over seven hundred pieces, prepared by a commission of nineteen, including one writer and four artists, headed by Lung Ta-yüan, president of the Board of Rites (*Li pu*) who also prefaced the work in 1176. . . . The second preface by Kiang Ch'un, dated 1779, relates how "a manuscript copy of the book had been purchased in 1773, when the Emperor had issued a decree to search throughout the empire for lost books, and a copy sent to be examined by the library commission then sitting."

Laufer then notes that he had studied the original manuscript of the last-named work and "found the description clearly written and the illustrations cleverly executed," and compared it with a work on bronzes, the *Po ku t'u.* While the latter was printed and several times reprinted, the *Ku yü t'u p'u* for some reason remained in manuscript form, "and attracted no notice, not being included in the *Catalogue of Literature* of the Sung History, nor quoted by older writers."[2] He goes on to join with Bushell in condemning the work as containing "a great deal of suspicious matter," but "while it is entirely untrustworthy for archaeological studies, it has a certain value in presenting a grammar of ornaments and giving the names for these, as they were current in the Sung period."

The *Ku yü t'u p'u* was criticised in an official publication of 1789, and declared to be a forgery. Bushell and Laufer both ignored this verdict, but modern writers accept it and Professor Hansford has summed up his own conclusions and those of his contemporaries in *Chinese Jade Carvings.*[3]

> 4. *Ku yü t'u k'ao*—*Investigations into Ancient Jades with Illustrations,* in two quarto volumes, published in 1889 by the well-known scholar and statesman, Wu Ta-ch'êng, who was born in Su-chou in 1833. . . . In his work on jades, two hundred and fifteen pieces are illustrated in outline, as a rule reduced to seven-tenths of their original size, described as to their colouring, identified with their ancient literature, among which *Chou li, Li ki, Shi king, Tso chuan* and the dictionary *Shou wên* are conspicuous.

Laufer records his great indebtedness to Wu whose approach to the subject "is not bound by the fetters of the past." He states: "I have followed him with keen admiration and stand to him in the relation of a disciple to his master."[4]

In his 370-page book Berthold Laufer strove nobly to pick his way through the accumulated misconceptions and fictions of several centuries, and to identify and date the early jade that came to his notice. It was a daunting task. The majority of pieces were without documentation of any kind and each had to be judged purely on visual evidence. Those pieces with a pedigree usually boasted one that did not withstand investigation. Written records were notoriously inexact and grew further confused in translation, while the drawings were usually as ambiguous as the descriptions.

Much old jade exhibits few signs of wear because its hardness enables it to withstand a considerable amount of handling. As it normally reveals little or no indication of usage, dating must rely on external factors. One of the most certain of these, when it can be ascertained, lies in the circumstances of the finding of a specimen. When it is known that a certain piece came from a particular tomb of which the occupant has been identified, there can be little doubt that objects placed with the body predate the burial. That is, provided all has remained un-touched since the day of interment—a state of affairs that does not always occur.

The custom of furnishing the dead with a number of everyday objects is of long standing in China, as it was in other civilisations such as that of ancient Egypt. In China the practice goes back at least to the Shang dynasty. At that time it was thought that the high-born were possessed of twin souls, one of which, known as a *kuei* or ghost, remained in or about the tomb and required material comforts similar to those enjoyed by its possessor in his lifetime. The soul or spirit, a *shên*, was a more intellectual manifestation, and after death joined the similar souls of deceased members of the family.

The more worldly *kuei* required food and drink, vessels from which to partake of them, and all the apparel and trappings of daily life. At first both human and animal sacrifices formed part of the burial ceremony, but during the Chou period they were replaced by models made of pottery or some other suitable material. The more exalted the rank of the deceased person, the more costly and extensive was the array of material offerings supplied to serve the needs of, and to placate, the *kuei*. Some of the objects were of jade, and while a proportion were those used by the deceased when alive, others were made especially for the occasion. Just as in ancient Egypt where tombs were stocked with artifacts of daily use and of special mortuary type, from which something has been learned of life in those distant times, so in China the age and range of jades can be deduced from the contents of the tombs of those people who were interred in similar fashion.

These circumstances, combined with the well-known Chinese reverence for the dead and their tombs, would seem to be ideal for the archaeologist. But in China as elsewhere, there were always a small number of people who had fewer scruples than the majority of their compatriots. Over many centuries, successive generations of grave robbers have broken into tombs, making chaos of the contents, removing whatever they thought valuable, and making the work of modern archaeologists infinitely more difficult than it would otherwise have been.

The Swedish engineer Orvar Karlbeck, who spent much of his lifetime building railways in China and returned to the country in search of antiquities, wrote with firsthand knowledge of what was going on there in 1929. In the area of Huihsien, midway along and just off the main route of the Peking-Hankow railway line, he noted: "We did, in fact, come upon a number of tumuli, of which some were shaped like truncated pyramids. Almost all had been broken into and looted of their contents. This was never done openly lest the *hsienchang* [local governor] should intervene, and before the work began the mound was sown with kaoliang [sorghum grass]. When this had grown tall and thick enough to provide cover, a vertical shaft was dug, just wide enough to admit a man of normal girth. If anything of value was found, tunnels were thrown out from it in all directions. The digging took time, of course, but during the autumn and winter no work is done in the fields and the peasants are therefore unoccupied. When the grave was thought to have been emptied of its treasures the shaft was usually, though not always, filled in again."[5]

Some miles away from Huihsien, at Anyang, which had been the capital of the country in about 1300 B.C., the government-sponsored Academia Sinica carefully explored the site. Meanwhile, at a convenient distance from this activity the local inhabitants took the law into their own hands: "Looting of ancient graves was severely punished, sometimes even by death, and therefore the digging had to be done surreptitiously. The peasants could not understand why they should be forbidden to dig on their own land: it belonged to them, they said, with everything in it and under it. But during the period of the Empire they had learnt to 'tremble and obey.' Nowadays they trembled and disobeyed. The work had to be done after dark, and at twilight fifty or so men would set off, some armed with rifles, others with picks and shovels. The burial sites were guarded by the armed men, who fired upon anyone incautious enough to approach. The rest dug their way down into the grave, which might lie at a depth of 16 or 20 feet [4.5 to 6 metres] below the surface."[6]

Bronzes, jade, and other articles excavated under such circumstances were disposed of quickly and in secrecy, often to agents of dealers in Peking and elsewhere who waited patiently in nearby villages. Questions were rarely asked, and if they were it was doubtful if a truthful answer could, or would, be given. The genuineness of the goods was seldom doubted, for the peasants were only very rarely skillful or knowledgeable enough to make convincing forgeries. These were more likely to emanate from the cities, where they would be displayed innocently as part of a "find."

It is not at all unknown for goods to be buried deliberately in order to deceive an eager excavator. It has been reported that this was done for the benefit of Charles Lang Freer, the wealthy Detroit maker of railway carriages, who formed a very large collection of Oriental works of art, now in the Freer Gallery of Art, Washington, D.C. He visited China in 1907 to augment his accumulation of pottery, and decided he would like to pay a visit to some of the excavations whence much of it had come. This was easily arranged against payment in dollars, and the expedition set off into the country. Once there, Freer had the excitement and pleasure of disinterring some pottery figures, but duly discovered that the entire operation had been mounted especially for his gratification: both the grave and its contents were forgeries.

Despite so many pitfalls, experts of many countries have slowly managed to winnow the wheat from the chaff, and while the picture is by no means a complete one, it is gradually becoming more distinct. No doubt when China again allows free access to Westerners, there will be considerable advances in our knowledge of the subject of jade. Until then, we must be content with reading and interpreting the information printed from time to time in journals published in Peking and elsewhere, and with continuing to study the immense quantity of jade already in Europe and America.

There is little question but that the stone was accorded respect from the very earliest times, and for this reason it is doubtful whether, in spite of its hardness, it was ever formed into tools for actual use. While its hardness might have seemed to recommend it for practical purposes, it tended to be brittle, and many other types of stone, readily available in the country, were easier to work into satisfactory shapes and could more quickly be given a cutting edge. Almost all specimens of early jade, therefore, are symbolic in shape, ornamentation, and use. To investigate and consider their origins and significance is one of the more fascinating aspects of Oriental art.

The names and uses of the various types of ancient jades were given in the *Chou li* (The Rites of Chou) a book purporting to describe the ceremonial adjuncts of the Chou period. The work was not compiled until the end of the period, by which time it is not improbable that much had changed and memories had grown dim. Considerable use of this source was made by Laufer, but modern commentators are less inclined to accept it so freely; they do not suggest that the *Chou li* was necessarily written with dishonest intent, but rather that it records idealised hearsay with the gaps made good by guesswork.

Comparable doubts have been expressed concerning the few other remaining documents of the period, all of which were ordered to be destroyed in 213 B.C. when the Ch'in emperor attempted to efface records of previous rulers and customs. Fragments of some of those records escaped the holocaust, were later transcribed, and had added to them a proportion of later matter. The interpolations together with the archaic language of the whole make their elucidation both difficult and debatable.

According to the *Chou li,* a master of religious ceremonies, *ta tsung po,* had charge of certain important jade objects: "He makes of jade the six objects to do homage to Heaven, to Earth, and to the Four Points of the Compass. With the round tablet *pi* of bluish (or greenish) colour, he does homage to Heaven. With the yellow jade tube *ts'ung,* he does homage to Earth. With the green tablet *kuei,* he renders homage to the region of the East. With the red tablet *chang,* he renders homage to the region of the South. With the white tablet in the shape of a tiger (*hu*) he renders homage to the region of the West. With the black jade piece of semicircular shape (*huang*) he renders homage to the region of the North."

In addition, there are details of pieces placed in the coffin of a deceased member of the imperial household. They were superintended by the steward of the treasury, *t'ien fu,* of whom it was recorded in the *Chou li*: "He fastens silk cords through the apertures with which these six pieces are perforated. These are the *kuei,* the half-*kuei* or *chang,* the circular disc *pi,* the jade tube *ts'ung,* the tablet in shape of a tiger *hu,* and the tablet in shape of a half-circle *huang.* He removes the circular disc *pi* from the tube *ts'ung.* These objects are thus arranged to be deposited with the corpse in the coffin. . . . When the body is placed in the coffin, the *kuei* is to the left, the half-*kuei* is at the head. The tablet in the shape of a tiger is to the right. The tablet in shape of a half-circle is at the feet. The circular disc is under the back. The jade tube *ts'ung* is on the abdomen."[7]

While this particular ceremony is not mentioned in other records, the various objects listed in it and in the preceding extract have been identified. They vary in size and shape, as well as in the amount of ornamentation they bear, and in their age. Only a small proportion of extant specimens can be traced to datable tombs, and most of them were found or "appeared" prior to the advent of controlled excavations.

The principal ritual jades enumerated in the extracts quoted above from the *Chou li,* so far as can be determined in the light of present knowledge, are as follows:

The *kuei* were the symbols of authority of the five grades of nobility, *kung, hou, po, tzu,* and *nan,* roughly equivalent to duke, marquess, earl, viscount, and baron. They were carried on ceremonial occasions and varied in size and shape according to the rank of the holder. Each took the form of a flat tablet resembling a blunt knife blade, and was drilled with a hole at one end. It is argued that the references to such articles in ancient literature may not mean that they were necessarily made of jade, and that if they were, they would have been limited in numbers and therefore unlikely to have been buried with a nobleman on his death. More probably, it is thought, they would have been returned to the person who bestowed them on the dead man, or they would perhaps have passed to the person who succeeded him in his title.

The half-*kuei* or *chang* was, presumably, a small-sized *kuei,* and was perhaps worn suspended from the owner's girdle or belt. Three types of *chang* are recorded in the *Chou li: ta* meaning great; *chung,* middle; and *pien,* side. Laufer quotes one Chinese authority who stated that "these three *chang* are in reality basins to hold aromatic wine." But Laufer fails to comment on this apparently outlandish interpretation, and contents himself with illustrating a jade tablet that is rectangular in outline but cut at an angle at one end, bearing on one side an incised ornament, with its undecorated portion pierced with a hole. Laufer goes on to discuss the variety of *chang* named *ya chang,* suggesting that this is "the tablet *chang* with a tooth which serves to mobilise troops and to administrate the military posts." This statement infers that anyone bearing a *chang* of this type was empowered to raise an army and command it, a function comparable in a way to the modern field marshal's baton. The illustration in Laufer shows a knifelike blade, broadening and curved at one end, pierced with a hole at the other. On one edge, above the hole, is a raised projection resembling a tooth.

"The circular disc *pi*" is the best known of all the ancient jade objects, and takes the form of a flat circular plaque with a central hole. A dictionary compiled in the third or second century B.C. noted that if the stone portion is twice the

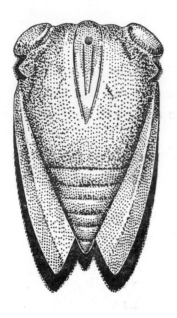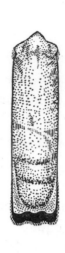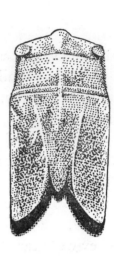

2. Cicada forms in tomb jades.

width of the perforation the object is a *pi;* if the proportions are reversed (i.e., the hole is twice as wide as the jade ring) it is a *yüan;* and if both measurements are about equal it is a *huan.*

The *pi* has a lengthy history, and its significance has given rise to considerable discussion. Its resemblance in shape to the sun, and the fact that the ancient Chinese character for the latter is a *pi,* suggest that it is a symbol of solar power. By analogy it would represent heaven and the very source of human life. It has been pointed out, however, that the statement "the *pi* is round and symbolises heaven" was not made until the second century A.D.; at least two thousand years after the first known examples of the object were made. Simple tool forms were without doubt the basis of all the ancient jades, but this particular one appears to have had no such obvious origin. One modern writer, "in obedience to the unwritten law decreeing that all Western students of jade shall find something new to say about *pi,*" puts forward the idea that it may have been evolved from the flywheel used in giving a drill the required momentum.[8]

The *ts'ung* had been identified as a tube with a circular cavity, squared on the outside, and with a short round neck at either end. Examples vary in size, ranging from about seven centimetres to as much as fifty centimetres in height and from about three centimetres to fifteen centimetres in width. In some instances the outer surfaces are plain, but in most cases they have been cut into a series of ribs resembling the stone quoins of a building.

It was once thought that they had been "part of a chariot-wheel nave," and they were called that in the *Ku yü t'u p'u.* The origin of the description is apparently an

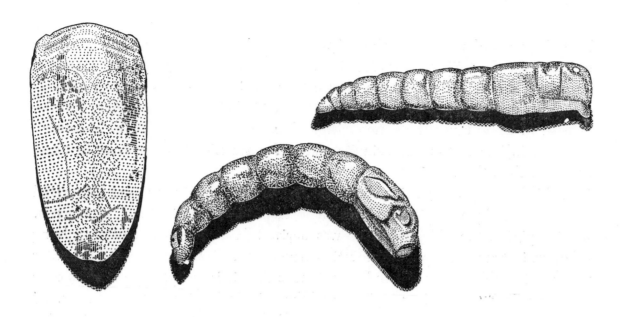

entry in a dictionary compiled in the second century A.D., where it is remarked that the *ts'ung* resembles a wheel nave. The key word "resembles" was duly altered and the two objects forthwith became one and the same thing; a state of affairs that lasted until Wu Ta-ch'êng published the result of his researches in 1889.

Laufer concluded that the *ts'ung* had a number of ritual uses. Primarily, as stated in the *Chou li,* it symbolised the earth, and when placed in a tomb it represented that deity. It was also the emblem of an empress; "a similar type was used by her as a scale weight, and if ever employed by the emperor it seems to be a secondary development by transfer from the female sphere, and there is no instance of his ever having made actual use of it in person. If offered as a token of respect by feudal princes, it was only presented by them to a princely consort. This emblem, therefore, has always referred to female power."[9]

In connexion with its use in burial, the *ts'ung* rested on the abdomen of the corpse, and together with the other emblems, the four quarters of the compass and heaven (*pi*), it implied that the deceased had with him in his afterlife the gods he had worshipped when living. Laufer considered that the *ts'ung* took the form of the Chinese conception of the earth, and in support of this he quoted the words of Liu Ngan, who died in 122 B.C.: "Heaven is round, and Earth is square; the principle of Heaven is roundness, and that of Earth squareness." The latter being "round in its interior and square on the outside."[10]

Another suggestion as to its origin was advanced in 1930 by Bernhard Karlgren, who thought the *ts'ung* had evolved from a container in which were kept the revered ancestral tablets of the country's rulers. At first a simple tube was used for the purpose, with four flat lengths of board or stone tied to it to stop its rolling about. The grooves in most extant specimens are, therefore, to be explained as vestiges of cuts made to prevent the binding cord from slipping off the boards. In Chou times the same written character represented both "ancestor" and "earth," so that it was a simple matter for the *ts'ung* to represent first one and then the other.

A third theory concerning the *ts'ung* was published in 1947 (and elaborated subsequently) by a Belgian engineer and astronomer, Henri Michel, of Brussels. In his opinion the object was, or was derived from, an astronomical sighting tube, an instrument for use in locating true north. Centuries ago the Pole Star was considerably less bright and conspicuous than it is today, and the skies over the Far East held no clear indicator of the principal point of the compass. By fitting over the *ts'ung* a serrated disc, also of jade and known as a *hsüan chi,* which was lined up on parts of the Great Bear and other constellations, "the position of the pole would then have been clearly indicated to the observer by looking through the *yü hêng* [or *ts'ung*]."[11]

Other writers have contributed yet further ideas on the subject, one of them, Edouard Erkes, amplifying Laufer's statement that the *ts'ung* was an emblem of female power. Erkes put forward in 1931 the idea that its "original meaning was that of an image of the Deity Earth, represented by her vagina, as the mother and bearer of all creatures." The Chinese character for earth was once a simplified representation of the phallus, so one may wonder where this line of speculation leads.

Other early jades take the form of spearheads and daggers, the spearheads sometimes retaining the bronze mounts, occasionally inlaid neatly with turquoises, by which they were fitted to wooden handles. Both weapons were almost certainly made of stone for ceremonial use only on court occasions, or in connexion with interment.

A further type of ritual jade remains to be mentioned; those pieces employed in burial and known variously as "mouth jades," "tomb jades," and *han yü;* the last term means literally "placed in the mouth" and not necessarily dating from the Han dynasty.

These small-sized jades played a part in Chinese beliefs concerning the dead. In the fourth century A.D. a Taoist philosopher, Ko Hung, stated: "If there is gold and jade in the nine apertures of the corpse, it will preserve the body from putrefaction." In part, the belief was founded on the quasi-embalming effect of

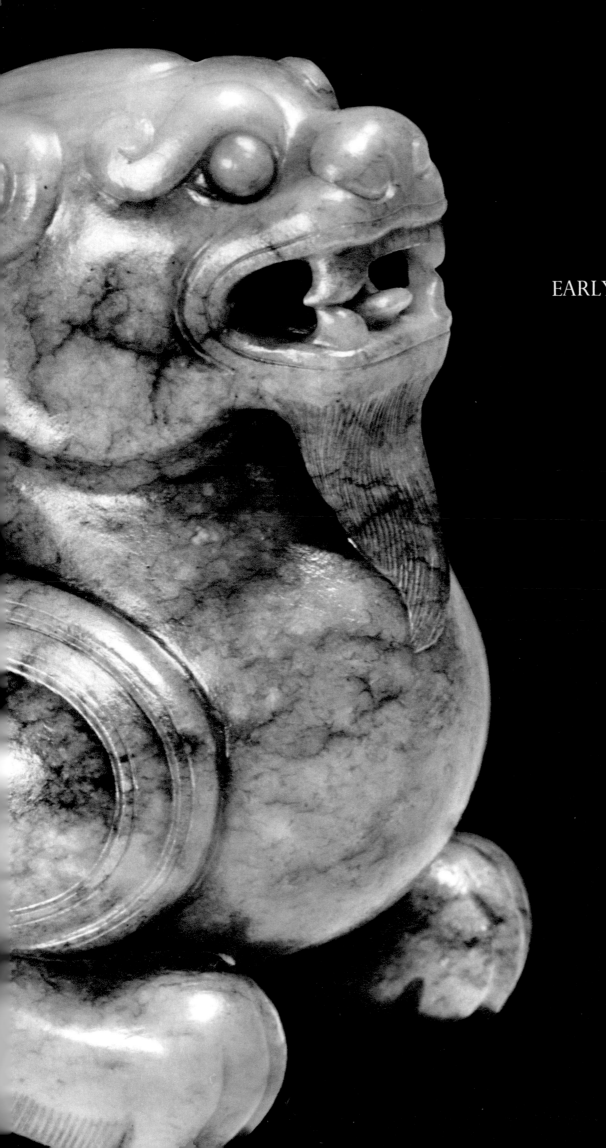

EARLY CHINESE JADE

Plates 6–51

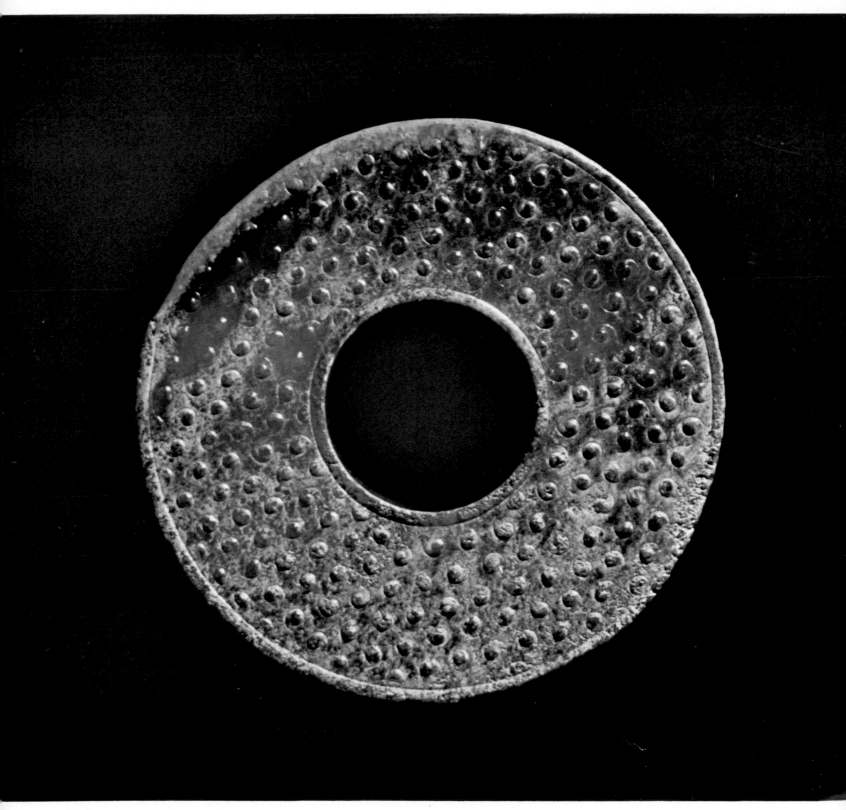

6. Pi. *Carved and incised on both sides with grain pattern within raised narrow borders. Surface disintegration. Late Chou dynasty. Diameter,* 9 cm. *Freer Gallery of Art, Washington, D.C.*

7. Ts'ung. *The horizontal bands are incised with archaic patterns. Surface decomposed. Chou dynasty. Height, 6.5 cm. Freer Gallery of Art, Washington, D.C.*

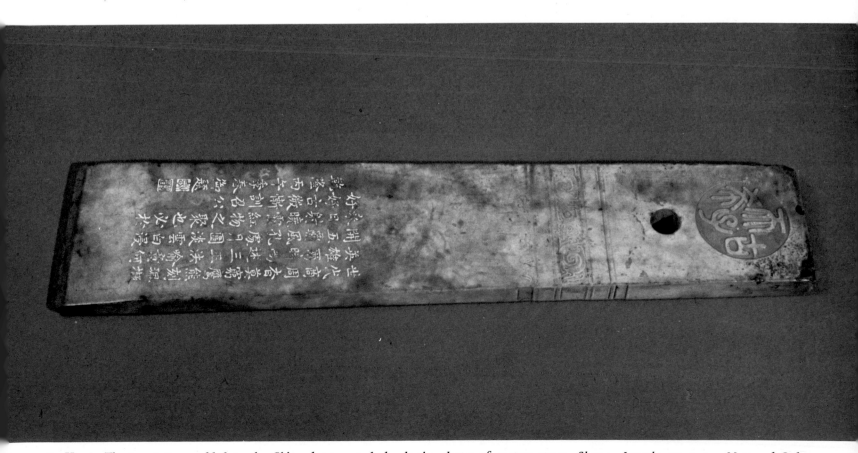

8. Kuei. *The inscription, added in the Ch'ien-lung period, lauds the glories of ancient times. Shang. Length, 31.5 cm. National Palace Museum, Taipei.*

9. Pi. *Carved and incised with a wide band of grain pattern within a border of stylised scroll-like dragons, and with narrow bands of rope pattern. Transparent green. Chou dynasty. Diameter, 30.2 cm. Metropolitan Museum of Art, New York. Rogers Fund, 1917. (This* pi *resembles in pattern one found at Loyang and now in the National Museum, Seoul; illustrated by S. H. Hansford,* Chinese Carved Jades, *1968, Plate 39a.)*

10. Pi. *Carved and incised with bands of conventional ▷ ornament separated by a narrow ridge of rope pattern. The reverse side bears a grain pattern. Mottled greenish white and pale brown with cream speckling. Late Chou dynasty. Diameter, 16.4 cm. Said to have been excavated in Shensi Province. Freer Gallery of Art, Washington, D.C.*

11. Pi. *Green with brown and silvery strata. Late Chou dynasty. Diameter, 21.7 cm. Freer Gallery of Art, Washington, D.C.*

12. *Incised, pierced ornament consisting of two stylised coiling dragons. Decomposed to light tan on one side and grey on the other. Late Chou dynasty. 7.7 × 2.3 cm. From Loyang. Freer Gallery of Art, Washington, D.C.*

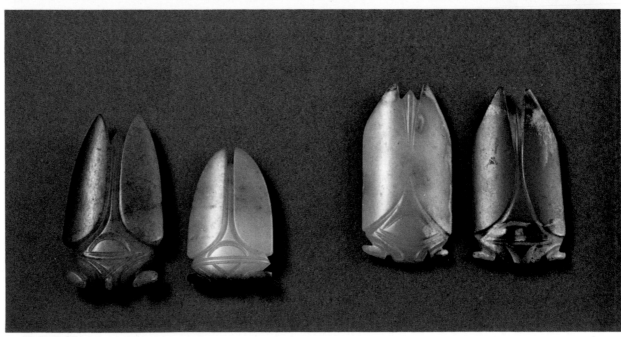

13. *Tomb jades in the form of cicadas. Han dynasty. Greatest length, 6.67 cm. National Palace Museum, Taipei.*

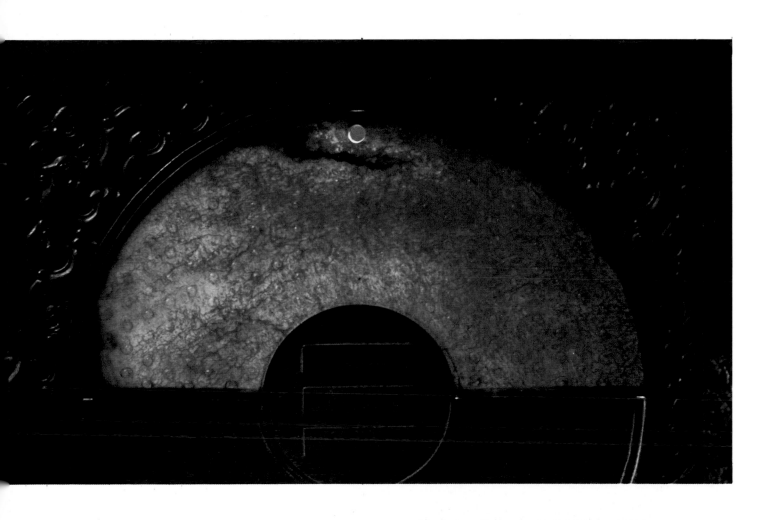

14-15. Huang. *Carved on both sides with grain pattern. Chou dynasty. Maximum measurement, 17.75 cm. National Palace Museum, Taipei.*

17. Ts'ung. *Mottled green and brown with patches of greyish disintegration. Chou dynasty. Height, 17.5 cm. Freer Gallery of Art, Washington, D.C.*

16. Ts'ung. *Mottled green and brown with traces of creamy decomposition. Attributed to Chou dynasty. Height, 20.7 cm. Freer Gallery of Art, Washington, D.C.*

18. *Ornament carved with grain pattern within incised interlocking spirals. At each end is a dragon's head. One perforation in centre. Cloudy-white decomposition on one side, but edges are noticeably sharp and the piece is highly polished. Late Chou dynasty. Length, 12.8 cm. From Loyang. Freer Gallery of Art, Washington, D.C.*

19–20. Detail and full view of ta-kuei, carved at one end with a stylised head. The outline of an animal is incised, and vestiges of an inscription remain. Mottled green, grey, and brown. Early Chou dynasty. Length, 72 cm.; greatest width, 18.3 cm. The head may be that of Chieh Kuei, a noted tyrant whose reign preceded the founding of the Shang dynasty. Freer Gallery of Art, Washington, D.C.

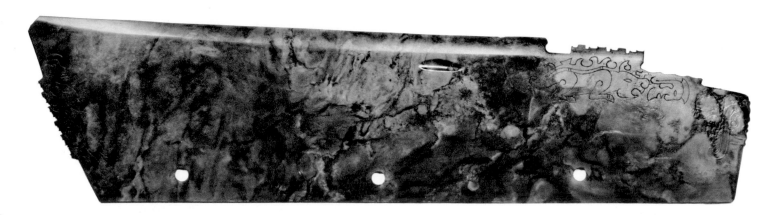

21. Ceremonial implement with a sharp, bevelled cutting edge, four perforations along one edge, and one towards the rounded end. Light green with cloudy-tan strata and scattered silvery markings. Shang dynasty. Length, 49.4 cm. Laufer illustrates a similar piece, describing it as an "Imperial Tablet hu for writing." Freer Gallery of Art, Washington, D.C.

22. Ceremonial implement perforated at one end. Translucent light and dark bluish grey. Shang dynasty. Length, 36.6 cm. Laufer described this and other similar pieces in a chapter entitled "Symbols of Sovereign Power." Freer Gallery of Art, Washington, D.C.

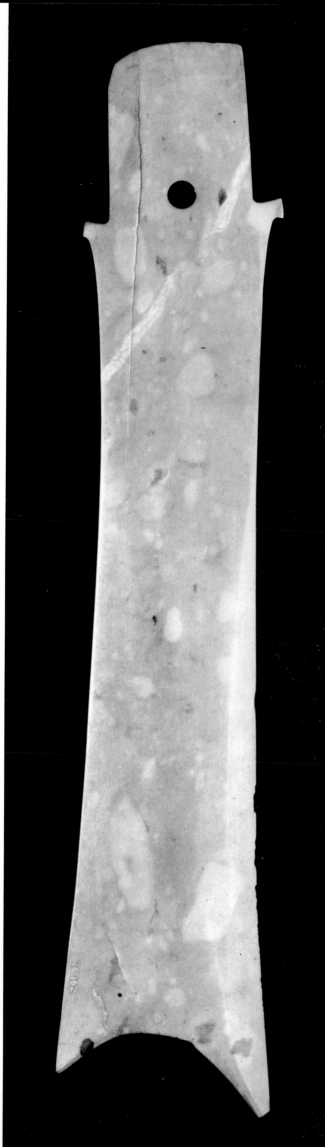

23. *Ornament with a dragon's head at each end, the tails forming spirals towards the middle, abutting on a "vase." The body is carved with grain pattern and pierced with two holes for attachment. Late Chou dynasty. Length, 11.2 cm. Freer Gallery of Art, Washington, D.C.*

24. *Ornament in the form of a birdlike creature. T'ang dynasty. 5.7 × 5 cm. Freer Gallery of Art, Washington, D.C.*

25. *Scabbard fitting (peng), carved with a long-tailed monster. Han dynasty. Width, 5.1 cm. National Palace Museum, Taipei.*

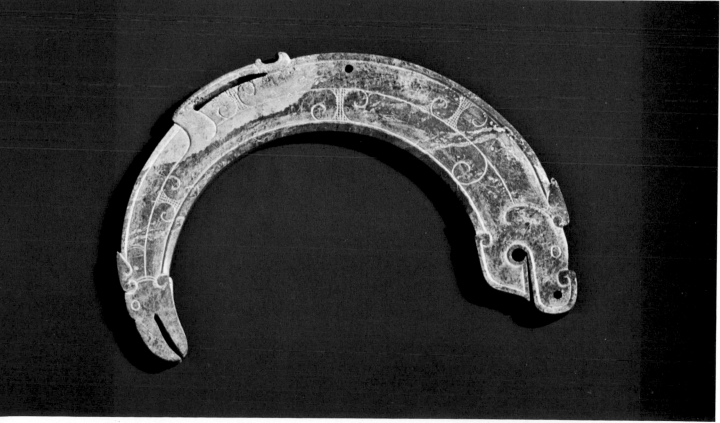

26. *Ornament, incised and carved in the form of a stylised creature whose one extremity is a dragon while the other appears to be a bird's head. Decomposed to grey and tan. Late Chou dynasty. Diameter, 9.5 cm.; greatest width, 2.1 cm. From Loyang. Freer Gallery of Art, Washington, D.C.*

27. *Halberd. Off-white ivory colour, the ridged end covered with gold. Shang dynasty. Length, 11.7 cm. Stated to have been found in a tomb in Honan Province. Metropolitan Museum of Art, New York. Fletcher Fund, 1925.*

28. *Ceremonial implement. Blade of mottled green-and-brown jade set in a handle of bronze inlaid with fragments of turquoise, and hollowed to take a shaft. Late Shang dynasty. Overall dimensions, 21.3 × 7.9 cm. Reported to have been found at Anyang. Freer Gallery of Art, Washington, D.C.*

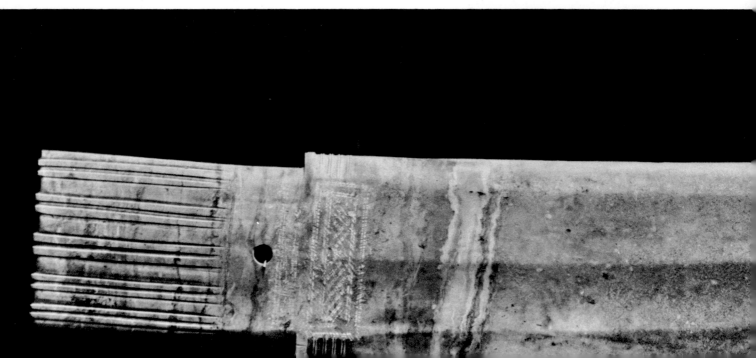

29. Kuei. *Mottled dark green with iridescent patches and areas of dull red. Chou dynasty. Length, 22.6 cm. Freer Gallery of Art, Washington, D.C.*

30. *Halberd (ko), carved and incised with parallel ridges and linear patterns. Opaque, mottled, and striped grey and yellow grey. Shang-Chou dynasties, circa twelfth century* B.C. *Length, 84.1 cm. In Plate 9 in* Jade *Laufer describes this piece as a dagger, and records it as in the possession of Tuan Fang of Peking, adding, "Its substance is a peculiar light reddish jade, such as I have seen in no other specimen, designated by the Chinese hung pao yü." He gave the length as 92 cm. Freer Gallery of Art, Washington, D.C.*

31. *Anthropomorphic case made of jade plaques held together with gold wire. Two such cases were discovered by Chinese archaeologists and the discovery was first published in 1971. The cases belonged to a prince and his wife of the Western Han period, about 110 B.C., and were discovered in a tomb said to resemble an underground palace that was equipped with vessels of bronze, and with gold, silver, and jade objects, lacquer, and silks. The jade cases have now been restored and are on display in Peking. Photograph by Marc Riboud, Magnum.*

32–33. Necklace of beads and carved ornaments assembled on braided gold wire. Green, decomposed in places to a whitish colour. Late Chou dynasty. Height, 40.7 cm. From Loyang. Freer Gallery of Art, Washington, D.C.

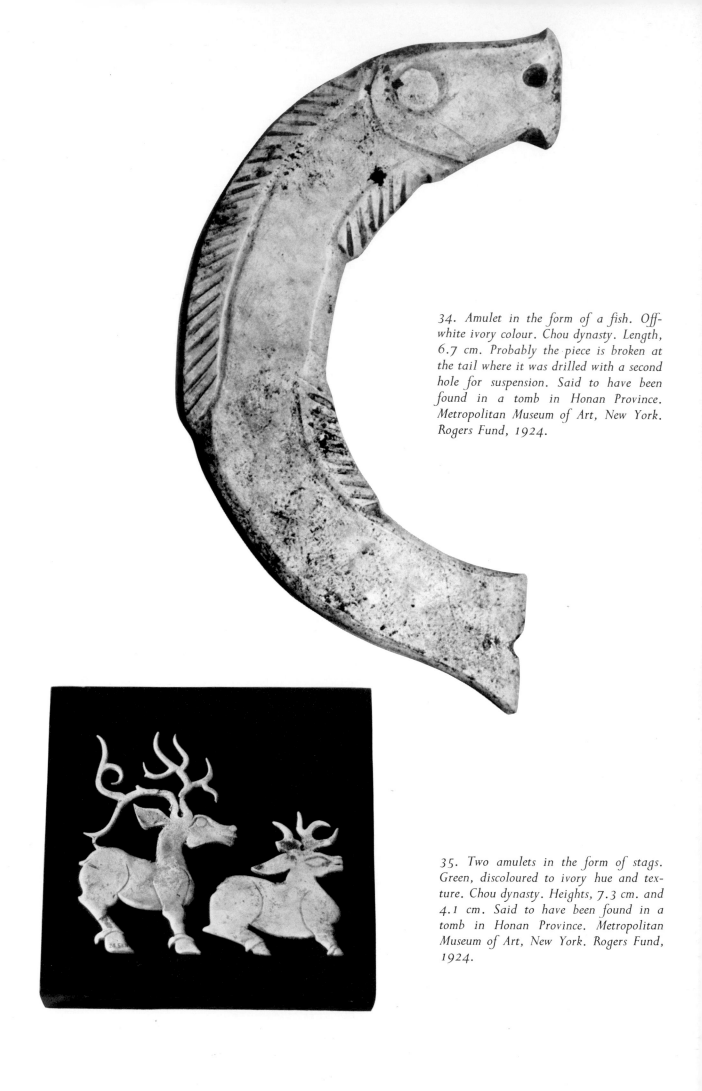

34. Amulet in the form of a fish. Off-white ivory colour. Chou dynasty. Length, 6.7 cm. Probably the piece is broken at the tail where it was drilled with a second hole for suspension. Said to have been found in a tomb in Honan Province. Metropolitan Museum of Art, New York. Rogers Fund, 1924.

35. Two amulets in the form of stags. Green, discoloured to ivory hue and texture. Chou dynasty. Heights, 7.3 cm. and 4.1 cm. Said to have been found in a tomb in Honan Province. Metropolitan Museum of Art, New York. Rogers Fund, 1924.

36. Ornament in the form of a mask with central vertical hole, and pierced in the back with six more holes. Chou dynasty. 4.6 × 4.1 cm. Freer Gallery of Art, Washington, D.C.

37–38. Two views of brush pot carved with dragons. Sung dynasty. Height, 16 cm. National Palace Museum, Taipei.

59

39–40. *Front and back of plaque, carved and pierced, in the form of a conventionalised tiger, the body decorated with grain pattern and spirals on both sides. Greenish white flecked with tan; cream coloured and blackish brown decomposition. Late Chou dynasty. 2.3 × 7.7 cm. From Loyang. Freer Gallery of Art, Washington, D.C.*

41. *Crouching tiger. Sung dynasty. Length, 18.4 cm. Somerset de Chair, Essex, England. (See page 41 for detail.)*

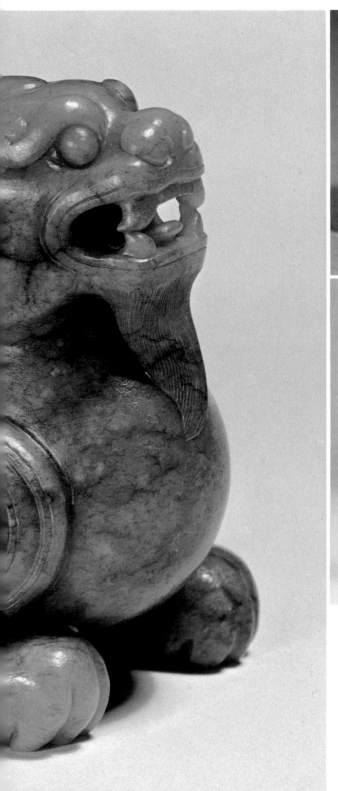

42. *Winged monster with mane and curled tail. T'ang dynasty. Length, 12 cm. National Palace Museum, Taipei.*

43. *Brush rest in the form of a shepherd seated on the rump of a ram. Han dynasty. Height, 11.5 cm. National Palace Museum, Taipei.*

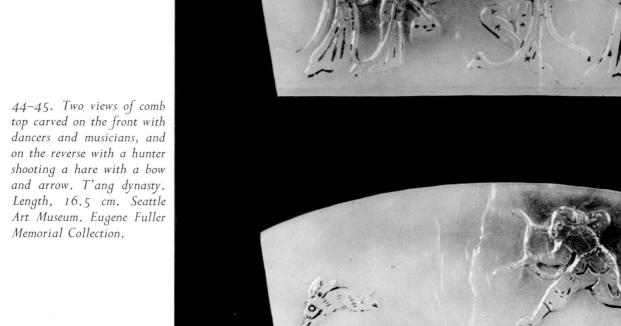

44–45. *Two views of comb top carved on the front with dancers and musicians, and on the reverse with a hunter shooting a hare with a bow and arrow. T'ang dynasty. Length, 16.5 cm. Seattle Art Museum. Eugene Fuller Memorial Collection.*

46. *Figure of a man with folded arms. Creamy white. Han dynasty. Height, 3.5 cm. Nelson Gallery, Atkins Museum, Kansas City.*

47. *Cup and cover, the body carved with stylised birds on a rice-grain ground. The feet of the cup descend from* t'ao t'ieh *masks. The cover has three ducklike figures. Pale green with brown areas. Late Chou dynasty. Over-all height, 17.1 cm. Freer Gallery of Art, Washington, D.C.*

◁ 48. Horse's head. Han dynasty. Height, 17.1 cm. Somerset de Chair, Essex, England.

49. Ornament, carved, pierced, and incised with a dragon's head at each end, and with a band of scroll design at the lower border of the main body that is covered with grain pattern. Grey. Late Chou dynasty. Length, 14.2 cm. Freer Gallery of Art, Washington, D.C.

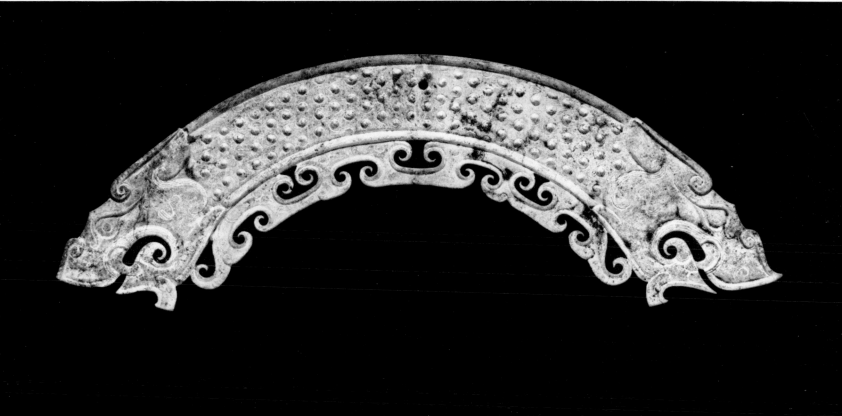

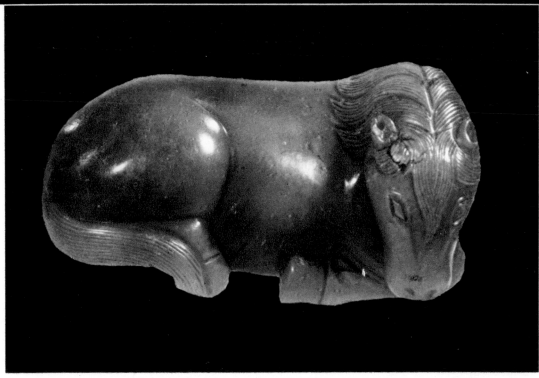

50. Recumbent pony. Yellow green. Yuan dynasty. Length, 6.3 cm. Christie's, London. From the Northwick Collection: Captain E. C. Spencer Churchill, M.C.

51. *Cup with a band of grain pattern. Brown. Perhaps Sung dynasty. Length, 14 cm. Metropolitan Museum of Art, New York. Bequest of Edmund C. Converse, 1921.*

sealing the apertures, and in part on the conviction that gold and jade were beneficial in themselves. In this connexion jade was recommended as a medicine in order to prolong life, although how the human digestion coped with the substance, even if it was swallowed in powder form, can scarcely be imagined.

The most important of the jades was the one placed in the mouth of the dead person. It was shaped roughly to the outline of the tongue, and frequently carved to represent a cicada, the long-lived insect common in the Far East and elsewhere. The fact that after hatching, the young penetrate deep into the earth and eventually emerge as winged adult cicadas, led the Chinese to compare the process to resurrection. In the words of one of the numerous philosophers, "The vital spirit of a dead man leaving the body may be compared to the cicada emerging from the chrysalis."

The same series included oval or curved pieces for placing over the eyes, the latter carved to represent fishes—symbols of "watchfulness." Others are short rods, sometimes faceted and tapered along their length or bearing simple geometrical patterns, and intended for insertion in the orifices of the torso. In some instances the various pieces are drilled with small holes, in the case of the eye covers presumably for tying them in position.

Finally, the shroud covering the body was most carefully disposed in folds, held in place by small weights of carved jade. Occasionally, the face beneath the shroud was further protected by a "veil" in the shape of a series of a dozen or so jade plaques, linked by silk cords shaped to suggest the unseen features.[12]

So far, consideration has been given to the jade articles with ritual significance —objects that played their parts in various ceremonies connected with religion and the court. The use of the material was not limited, however, to such occurrences as funerals and state occasions, and jade was also employed for more mundane purposes. For these, it was confined to the affluent who were able to afford its high cost, and largely to those who combined the ownership of wealth with the sensitivity to appreciate the beauty of the stone.

As early as the Shang dynasty, jade carvers were sufficiently skilled to be able to cut the material into sections no more than a few millimetres thick. From these they fashioned pendants and plaques, of which some, it is conjectured, were sewn to clothing or inset in metal objects and furniture, while others were linked together with silk cords or gold chains to form breast ornaments. The small-sized plaques are almost indistinguishable from those used for burial "veils," and many of the shapes in which both occur are the same.

Laufer reprinted from the *Ku yü t'u p'u* what he described as an "Ancient Jade

Girdle-Pendant," and the illustration shows a group of seven pieces of jade linked by what might be either lightweight chains or a series of cords on which beads are threaded. Although he admitted that the illustration was "not correct in details, and nothing more than an attempt at reconstruction,"[13] Laufer went on to identify a series of jades that more or less matched those depicted. They are, in fact, no different in appearance from pieces that may have been sewn to clothing, or composed into breast ornaments (pectorals) and burial "veils." Thus it is only very rarely possible to be certain of the precise purpose for which many surviving jades of the kind were made.

Jade was sometimes used to make ornamental fittings for swords and scabbards, and for the device by which the weapon was suspended from a belt. The belt or girdle was further embellished with plaques, and could be fastened by means of a pair of hooks. These were often made entirely of jade, although examples are recorded made of gold, silver gilt, and gilded bronze inset with pieces of jade.

One property of the stone has not yet been mentioned: its quality of resonance. The compact nature and durability of jade enable it to be used in the form of a simple musical instrument. Laufer described how these are of two different types: ". . . the single stone and the compound stones. The former (t'ê k'ing) is a stone cut somewhat in the shape of a carpenter's square, but in the form of an obtuse angle with two limbs, the longer one called the 'drum,' the shorter, the 'limb.' It is suspended in a wooden frame by means of a silk cord passing through a hole bored at the apex. It is still employed during the ceremonies performed in the Confucian temples and struck with a hammer against the longer limb to give a single note at the end of each verse. In the compound stones (pien king), sixteen of the same type as the single stone, but on a smaller scale, are suspended in two equal rows on a wooden frame, all being of the same dimensions in length and breadth, differing only in thickness; the thicker the stone, the deeper the sound. Also this instrument serves in the Confucian temples, in connexion with bell-chimes, the bell being struck at the beginning of each long note in the tune, and the stone at the end."[14]

Apart from being used in this manner, pieces of jade were worn suspended on the person so that they tinkled with the movement of walking. According to one authority, the stones on the right-hand side gave forth one set of notes, and those on the left another. One of the justifications of this continual musical accompaniment was that it kept at bay any evil or depraved thoughts otherwise likely to occupy the mind. The sound was equated with happiness so the pendants were not worn during periods of mourning, and an heir apparent was forbidden to let them sound when in the presence of the emperor. It must have been a refreshingly pleasant world in which a victorious general was remembered because of "the tinkling of the bells of his horses and the sounding of the gems of his girdle-pendants."

DECORATIONS AND PATTERNS

IN THE preceding section attention was paid to the principal types of ancient jades, and at the same time their actual and, in some cases, probable uses were discussed. It now remains to describe the designs employed in shaping and ornamenting them.

Mention has already been made of the first attempts to date jade pieces by reference to such old documents as were available. While these often provided some clues, they seldom told the whole truth, and the many so-called facts they contained tended to be the deductions of writers living long after the articles in question were made and had fallen into disuse. Error was piled on error as one writer copied from the "facts" of another, and it was not until the very end of the nineteenth century that there were any really serious attempts to disentangle fact from fiction.

Berthold Laufer added considerably to knowledge of the subject in 1912, but he, too, had to make guesses where he was unable to trace a credible source of information. In some cases he accepted statements that have been discredited by subsequent writers, but on the other hand much of his work remains valid after more than half a century. There can be no doubt that he was subjected to the same perils that beset anyone inquiring into the affairs of the Far East. More so than in other parts of the globe, the inhabitants of the Orient guard their secrets from strangers, striving to keep outsiders at a distance. The French Jesuit missionary, Father le Compte, wrote that from the earliest times the Chinese race "laid down a Maxim of State amongst themselves, To have no Commerce with Foreigners and Strangers, but just so much as should be necessary to receive their Homages."[15]

The attitude is well exemplified in the dealings of the Chinese with the representatives of the East India Company, who came to buy tea, silk, porcelain, and other goods in exchange for good silver money. The European traders were confined mostly to the use of the single port of Canton, chosen because it was the farthest situated from the capital at Peking. They could do business only with certain Chinese merchants, known collectively as the Hong, and were confined strictly to the waterfront area where their warehouses were situated. The trade was almost entirely one way and therefore to the great benefit of the Chinese. Yet the Chinese continually harried the foreigners. The habits transmitted from one generation to another proved to be long-lived, and even during periods of apparent liberalisation the caution exercised over many centuries remained unabated.[16]

Not only was Laufer working in a land where reliable information was hard to gain, but he was trying to acquire knowledge of a subject that had been examined by very few Westerners. In some measure he was like a man in a strange countryside where the inhabitants have removed or interchanged the signposts. Additionally, he had money to spend, and this fact, which would doubtless have been spread abroad with speed, also brought forth the unscrupulous. This would have been the case especially in areas distant from the large towns, where a blend of ignorance and cupidity tended to override any inclinations to honesty.

Aided by cunning makers of forgeries, the peasants would attempt to sell a potential buyer as much as he wanted to purchase. More dangerous still, they would invent and tell him whatever they thought might be to their advantage in such transactions. As soon as it was known that excavated pieces were being sought, they would be produced in company with evidence sufficient to satisfy the most eager seeker after facts.

It seems probable, however, that Laufer was alive to these possibilities, for in writing about terracotta mortuary figures he warns his readers: "The complete finds have naturally been rare, and in most cases masses of single heads and parts of the body have come to light which were then stuck together haphazardly by inventive Chinamen or even completed with additional clay substances in the hope of an increase in price from the prospective sale to the foreigner."[17]

Laufer depended mainly on literary sources: the discredited *Ku yü t'u p'u,* and the well-intentioned *Ku yü t'u k'ao* of Wu Ta-ch'êng, which was published in 1889. Such sources had to be interpreted into modern language and translated into a European tongue. In some instances Laufer relied on the earlier work of French experts, and had to further translate what they had rendered from the original Chinese. Thus there is ample scope for divergences of opinion as to the significance of many of the key words, not to mention others of lesser importance. While some of those words have been defined and their meanings are generally accepted, a number of them have not been agreed on and probably never will be.

The numerous usages of the word *yü* by the Chinese provide a case in point. Not only does the character mean jade, but it can also indicate marble and various other decorative stones, according to the whim of the writer and prevailing custom. When translating the words of a long-deceased author it is not always an easy matter to determine whether he refers to jade, serpentine, or something else of the kind. *Yü* was employed also in a commendatory sense, so that *yü hsin* (jade heart) is a pure heart and *yü nü* (jade woman) refers both to fairies and to ladies of noble birth. It has been pointed out that the English use of the word "golden" provides a parallel with terms such as "golden rule," " heart of gold," and *The Golden Treasury*.[18]

Many of the illustrations in the *Ku yü t'u p'u* bear captions alleging that they depict jade articles dating from the Chou and Han dynasties. In fact, they show objects made of bronze in those and earlier periods, taken flagrantly from the *Po ku t'u* and *K'ao ku t'u,* catalogues of antiquities in imperial and private collections.[19] As these books are known only from editions published in the eighteenth century, they too must be used with circumspection. Successive printings undoubtedly wore out the woodblocks used for the illustrations, and the blocks were doubtless recut. It is not at all improbable that when this was done they were embellished at the cost of the character of the earlier work, and their usefulness as true records was thus considerably diminished.[20]

The linking of jade and bronze for purposes of study is less incongruous than may be thought, for the designs ornamenting these two very different materials have much in common, in spite of the fact that the techniques of craftsmanship involved are in no way related. While the motifs on jade were incised or ground into a flat surface, those on bronzes were modelled in the first place in a soft wax prior to being cast in metal. Such transfer of ornament, as well as of external shape and function, from one material to another is not unusual with the Chinese. It occurs over the centuries with porcelain, lacquer, enamel, glass, and rhinoceros horn, all or some of which were made to simulate most of the others in texture, form, and decoration.

Bronze objects were much more plentiful in the past than those of jade, and since a greater number of them have survived, to study them is of considerable value in relation to the study of jade. Within the last few decades a reliable sequence of dates for both bronze and jade has been slowly forming as a result of the systematic excavation of ancient burial sites. In the past, the appearance of bronzes, jades, and other objects from tombs was the result of straightforward robbery, and little or no reliance could be placed on the alleged provenance of the loot. Not only did the robbers and their agents intend to keep the real sources secret in case of competition from other robbers, but since the whole activity was illegal they were in danger of the thunder of official disapproval, and severe punishment.

The most important of the scientific excavations have centered on Anyang, formerly known as Chang-tê Fu, in the province of Honan, on the Peking–Han-kow railway. The story of the locating of the accumulation of objects, and their interpretation, took many years to unfold, but the results of careful digging and investigation have greatly widened knowledge of the history and culture of early China.

In the last years of the nineteenth century the inhabitants of a village about three kilometres outside Anyang began to find inscribed bones and tortoise-shells in the local fields. They had come to light possibly through the banks of a local river collapsing to reveal the long-buried objects, or as a result of random digging by peasants in search of valuables of any kind. The bones and shells were at first regarded as mere curios, and quantities of the former, known as "dragon bones," were disposed of to apothecaries to grind up and use as medicine.

In due course someone took notice of the unusual marks on the objects, and scholars became interested in them. It took about ten years before their source was located, for dealers and others took every care to keep the place secret. Eventually the source was found, and at the present time more than one hundred thousand bones and shells are known to have been unearthed. Since excavations are still in progress, the number is continually increasing.

As a result of careful research, it is now accepted that the bones and tortoise-shells are relics of the ancient practice of scapulimancy,[21] which involved the incising or painting of questions in written characters on animal bones or shells, the queries mostly being addressed to the spirits of the ancestors of a royal in-quirer, and dealing with everyday matters. After a hot tool had been applied to a prepared portion on the reverse side, a number of cracks developed and these were interpreted by a diviner who pronounced the answer to the original ques-tion.

Further investigations in the Anyang area brought to light the foundations of old buildings and a series of tombs, making it possible to confirm the local tradi-tion that the place had once been the site of the capital of the Shang dynasty (c. 1520–1030 B.C.). The oracle bones were of the same period, and had been used for the daily guidance of the Shang kings and their subjects. Carefully organised excavation began in 1927, and as a result of this and later work quantities of bones as well as bronzes and other artifacts were uncovered.

By painstakingly interpreting the characters on the bones and shells, Chinese scholars have been able to confirm that literary references to Shang kings, their names, and the order in which they reigned, were correct. The entire Shang dynasty had for a long while been considered by many to be a mere figment of scholarly imagination, but it was found that the oracle messages fall into five periods, so that their many queries cover a considerable length of time.

All this has been deduced in spite of the activities of nefarious people, both skilled and unskilled, who did not hesitate to cut invented texts on any undecorated bones that were unearthed. Comparable activities are recorded by Orvar Karlbeck, who visited the Anyang district several times, and wrote: "One man, perhaps, would take some ancient clay jar and try to make it more desirable by scratching on it a design which he imagined to be in the Yin [Shang] style, but without properly grasping the motifs. Another would bring a brand-new urn filled with earth, and declare it to be twelfth-century work. Again, a man might take an old bone—a dragon-bone—and make a vessel out of it. No one in his right mind would have been taken in by these things. But labour is cheap in China, and it did these fellows no harm to practice their carving."[22]

A large proportion of the items found in Honan are of bronze, and the considerable number of examples that are datable without doubt to the Shang dynasty has provided an unequalled opportunity for study. The decoration of the various articles has been examined, inscriptions have been read and translated, and the styles current during the period can now be recognised.

The significant feature of Shang and later decoration is a pre-occupation on the part of craftsmen with real and imaginary animal forms. Frequently they have been given highly elaborate treatment, the various elements composing a creature being ingeniously reshaped until they acquired an abstract appearance that now defies recognition. The counterpoint of such patterns is a challenge to the most expert, but like the music of, say, Bach, they can be enjoyed for their own sake by the uninitiated.

Typical bronze vessels excavated at Anyang have their surfaces ornamented with complex patterns of whorls and geometrical lines. In most instances these combine to form a series of masks, the eyes being indicated by studlike projections. Fearsome in appearance, the partial face (for it nearly always lacks a noticeable chin) is that of a monster and is known as a *t'ao t'ieh*.

The words in modern times mean "glutton," and it has been suggested that the appearance of the *t'ao t'ieh* on food vessels was a warning to the potentially greedy. Its precise origin and its significance in Shang times are unknown, despite many attempts to resolve the mystery. The masks mostly occur in two forms: bovine

3–4. Two types of t'ao t'ieh *masks from bronzes.*

5. A t'ao t'ieh *mask from a carved jade.* ▷

and feline. The former sometimes have their oxlike appearance modified by the addition of the fangs and claws of the latter. It has been argued that when found on the exterior of sacrificial vessels such decoration may well have indicated the contents. In the days when oxen, rams, and other animals were slaughtered for ritual purposes, and selected portions of the carcasses offered to the gods, certain vessels may well have been reserved especially for each species.

Among other living creatures adapted to the decoration of bronzes are tigers, elephants, snakes, deer, owls, fishes, and cicadas. They do not always appear in complete form, and deceptive abstractions are more commonly found. Birdlike heads with gaping beaks, which were possibly purely imaginary and decorative, are seen helping to fill spaces that might otherwise have remained blank.

Along with the bronzes excavated at Anyang, a large quantity of carved stones was found, of which a proportion was jade. Almost all are small in size, or fragments of larger objects—otherwise robbers would doubtless have removed them long ago. Thus the original appearance of many of the pieces can only be surmised.

Finds were also made at Loyang, in Honan Province, during the 1920s, but digging was carried out in a somewhat haphazard manner. No proper record was kept, and the value of the operation was therefore considerably diminished. Nonetheless, a number of museums have exhibits that are accepted as having come from the Chou dynasty tombs of Loyang; tombs that were described and illustrated by a visitor to the district, Bishop W. C. White.[23] He did not actually see the work while it was being carried out, and had to rely on the local inhabitants to tell him what had occurred and where the various pieces had been located.

Since then, many other excavations have taken place, but reports on them have not always been given in full, and both written descriptions and illustrations usually leave much to be desired. An exception is the detailed information on a tomb at Chengtu, in Szechwan, given by Dr. Michael Sullivan in 1948.[24] The excavation took place as a result of the chance finding of a brick wall when an air-raid shelter was being dug in 1939. Operations were eventually directed by the Academia Sinica and lasted the twelve months from September 1942 to September 1943, during which much time was consumed in carefully sifting the tons of mud that had percolated into the tomb over the centuries, engulfing that portion of the original contents which had not been removed earlier by the inevitable thieves.

The tomb was that of Wang Chien, self-proclaimed emperor of Ta Shu (A.D. 907–18). He lived during the T'ang period, and although not a truly royal personage, he was apparently treated as one by his subjects and was given a burial appropriate to the position he had taken. Whereas the influx of mud had rotted all but traces of woven fabrics, lacquer, and anything made of wood, such jade as remained was in good condition. The principal objects comprised some plaques from the emperor's belt, two books, each "consisting of fifty-three separate leaves of jade . . . strung together on silver wire," an engraved seal, and a *pi*.

The belt plaques, of white jade, were each carved with a dragon chasing a pearl, and included seven of square shape and one oblong. The latter bore on its reverse side an inscription, which recorded a fire that took place in the imperial palace on October 27, 915, and other matters. Both the book and the seal confirmed the name and status of the subject of the interment, and the former bore characters running vertically in a single line incised into the stone and gilded. Each leaf was approximately thirty-three centimetres long, and three centimetres wide, while the back and front "covers" were the same length, but some eleven millimetres wide.

Other excavations that have been made during the past few decades and recorded in Chinese journals are noted by Professor Hansford, and many are also to be found described and illustrated by William Watson in *Archaeology in China*, published in 1960. Activity continues, but it has been pointed out that so much of the past lies buried in Chinese soil, and present-day building activities are bringing so much of it to light, that books and articles are out of date almost before they are published. However, what is known already of the country and its arts is sufficient to enable a broad outline to be discerned. The detail also is present in many instances, and in others awaits the correction or confirmation of theories. Surprises continually come to light, new theories are advanced, accepted, and sometimes eventually rejected. Objects that are so rare as to be thought unique in one generation, are often discovered to be more plentiful than was suspected—or indeed hoped. This has now taken place with ancient jade representations of human beings.

In 1912, Laufer wrote that "in the ancient jades and bronzes the human figure is conspicuously absent. And the jade carving representing a human figure and ascribed to the Han period is the only exception of this kind." The figure he shows is of a man with rudimentary features, lacking nose and ears, on a triangular face, the point of the triangle downward and presumably representing the beard. His arms are folded across his body and he wears a long garment on which are indicated a few folds, while a flat hat is on his head. A somewhat similar man, but with the surfaces rounded and the whole figure even more stylised in conception, is in the Seligman Collection, belonging to the Arts Council of Great Britain, London. It is dated to the third century B.C., "Chou, perhaps Ch'u state."[25]

Since Laufer's time a number of human figures carved in jade have come to light. Most of them are stylised to a certain degree, possibly because the nature of the stone itself would make a perfect rendering on a small scale extremely difficult. A number of late Chou examples have been excavated at Loyang, and those illustrated in a Chinese journal include two figures of men seated on crouching animals. All of them measure between five and eight centimetres in height.

Perhaps the most striking of the Loyang finds is a series of ornaments wired to form a pectoral (an elaborate necklace), of which one part is in the form of a pair of female dancers. In contrast with most other surviving human representations of the period, the dancers are remarkably detailed, their hair and features being carefully rendered, and the folds of their dresses realistically incised to simulate movement. They depart from fidelity only where one arm of each figure rises from the upraised sleeve in the shape of a fluted sinuous curve to link at the top for suspension (Plates 32 and 33).

A later example than that just mentioned is shown in Plate 46 and is attributed to the Han dynasty. It spite of its tiny dimensions—it stands only thirty-five millimetres high—the maker has managed to incorporate considerable detail. But like most other human figures of jade made prior to the seventeenth century, the head springs from the body with a minimum of neck intervening.

Another kind of figure is typified by the head with grotesque features illustrated in Plate 36, which is paralleled by examples found in South America. Full-length figures with similar facial characteristics—flattened noses, prominent eyes, and protruding ears—are known, and are attributed to the Chou dynasty.[26]

While human figures in jade are now acknowledged to be less scarce than was once thought to be the case, animals are comparatively numerous. They range from the realistic and recognisable to those which are so stylised or representative of long-forgotten myths as to be unidentifiable. In many instances the portrayals combine not only the potential influence of the animal itself, but the mystical qualities with which the stone was endowed.

One of the most extensive mythologies is attached to the horse, whose tail, it is fancifully said, was imitated by the former Chinese habit of wearing pigtails "as a grateful tribute to the animal to which they owed so much."[27] In jade, the horse is found both as a complete animal and as the head only; of the latter, only a few specimens have been recorded and are of outstanding beauty.

The example now in the Victoria and Albert Museum, London, and formerly in the Eumorfopoulos Collection, must be familiar to hundreds of thousands of people who have visited the museum, and also from frequent reproduction.[28] It is in two parts, the head itself and the front portion of the body, the head slightly lowered and the neck arched to form an outstanding piece of sculpture. It is possible that the pose was dictated as much by the shape of the uncut stone as by the conception and tools of the carver.

Differently posed and less well known is the head illustrated in Plate 48. Attributed to an earlier date than the preceding specimen, it differs from it by being more stylised in the modelling, the form of the cheeks, and the notably distended nostrils giving a most striking appearance. The shape of the cheek goes back to the late Chou dynasty (sixth to third centuries B.C.), although it was employed in later times and therefore provides no real clue to dating. It is noteworthy that, like many of those in pottery, the head is shown with the jaws slightly apart revealing the canine teeth as well as the incisors—a feature characteristic of earlier rather than later examples.

In the same collection as this horse's head is the magnificent seated pony in Plate 52, which is the largest of its kind so far recorded. The carver has achieved a remarkable naturalism and has made the best use of a fine piece of stone for his chosen subject. In common with other pieces of high quality, the underside is as carefully and completely finished as the portions more usually visible (Plate 54).

Equally impressive is the figure of a water buffalo in Plate 77; an animal which is as popular with jade carvers as the horse. The shape of the recumbent beast lends itself particularly well to the material, although this is not to deny that considerable artistry and skill were required to produce a lifelike effect. This one, as well as a number of comparable figures, merits the words applied by J. P. Palmer to the example in the Fitzwilliam Museum, Cambridge: "By a series of subtle curved lines the body of the buffalo has been made to appear soft to the touch—one almost expects to see its body rise and fall as it breathes."[29]

Deer make occasional appearances in jade in the early Chou, when they were copied on a small scale and usually in silhouette on thin plaques. The animal is traditionally thought to be very long lived, and when it has reached a thousand years of age its horns are said to turn back, denoting that immortality has been attained. It is thus a symbol of long life, and the horns of real deer, suitably treated by drying and pulverising the various parts, are taken by the Chinese as a medicine in the attempt to increase the lifespan of the believer. Since the horn contains a considerable proportion of phosphate of lime, it would seem more likely to assist infants with rickets than to arrest senility.

While other animals including tigers and elephants have occasionally been noted, the majority of recorded specimens, either carved in the round or as flat plaques, are not to be identified directly with anything known to man, and are perhaps best described as "monsters." It has been pointed out that "The Eastern dragon is not the gruesome monster of medieval imagination, but the genius of strength and goodness. He is the spirit of change, therefore of life itself . . ." Apparently the dragon can render itself invisible at pleasure and has at its command all the tricks of a pantomime character. It is supposed to have nine forms, which differ both in their characteristics and in their appearance, but are seldom easy to identify. Some of the forms combine recognisable portions of real animals; such is the *lung-ma,* which has the body of a dragon with the legs of a horse. It is recorded as having appeared, along with the tortoise, before Emperor Hwang-ti

(c. 2650 B.C.) out of the waters of the Yellow River; is said to be "the first mention of the horse in Chinese mythology"; and also, to the bafflement of the modern reader, "a member of the crocodile family."[30]

The bands of diaper pattern, the hieroglyphlike scrolls, and similar designs that form a background of raised or incised decoration on many jades are often no less significant than animal forms. One of the more familiar of these patterns consists of a carpet of small raised dots, which is to be found ornamenting the rounded body of a bronze vase as well as the flat surface of a jade *pi* (Plate 6), when the latter becomes a *ku pi*. The small projections take two forms: simple and domed, and domed with curled or spiralling incisions springing from each. Both are usually described as "grain" pattern, because they are seen as formal representations of neatly arranged rows of rice, wheat, or other seeds. The curled variety is presumed to show the seeds sprouting through the earth, and thus to symbolise fertility. Either type must have been laborious to carve, and the perfection of some of the early examples, which can be dated to the first millennium B.C., indicates the high degree of skill attained by the craftsmen of the time.

Also found on the *pi* is the "rush" or "basket" pattern, which resembles woven cane with a crisscross of straight lines enclosing hexagonals and having the appearance of a honeycomb. When decorated in this manner, the *pi* is known as *p'u pi*. The symbolism embodied in this design seems to be uncertain, and possibly it may have been sufficient for the pattern to be purely decorative. Laufer thought it was the straightforward transference of a textile pattern to jade, but was less sure as to the reason for its adoption. He wrote: "Why was this design applied to the jade image of Heaven? A kind of rush called *shên p'u* is mentioned in the *Chou li* among the vegetable dishes presented to the Son of Heaven. This rush was plucked when it began to sprout in the water. The *Li ki* compares a prosperous administration with the rapid growth of rushes and reeds, and this may account for the employment of the ornament on the discs bestowed on the feudal lords of the fifth rank. On the other hand, rush baskets were used in ancient times to hold offerings for sacrifices, so that the rush-basket design on the images of Heaven may have well illustrated a sacrificial offering to the Deity."[31]

Other background designs were employed on fabrics as well as on bronzes and jades. The geometrical meander or "key" pattern is probably the most commonplace of them, and is familiar in European art as the Greek key or fret. The Chinese version is supposed to have had its origin in archaic representations of clouds and thunder, which in the course of time became combined into a single figure. Oriental agriculturalists were all too aware of their dependence on seasonal rain, which was not infrequently preceded by thunder, and the key pattern, or at least its origins, must have had great significance for them.

The foregoing are no more than a very few of the many shapes in which early jade exists, and some of the decorative details with which it was embellished. The fact that most of the forms and motifs are seen on pieces ranging in date over some three thousand years is one of the reasons for hesitating to date any one piece with certainty. Not only have the same patterns endured for such an extreme length of time, but this has occurred despite the innumerable upheavals with which the country has been continuously beset. Wars and civil wars divided and redivided the land of China, and yet the major part of its art symbolism has survived un-altered. In addition, the nature of jade precludes it from showing signs of wear that would be found on any other material. With jade, the passage of time has for the most part left few scars.

The continual Chinese reverence for the past has ensured the survival of much that would otherwise have been discarded, and it has also meant that careful copies of old favourites were deliberately made. While most of those produced in the past were not intended to deceive, the same can rarely be said of copies of modern date. The comparatively simple workmanship of many archaic pieces has proved an irresistible temptation to many people, but fortunately their artistic knowledge is usually on a par with their craftsmanship and the forgeries are im-mediately apparent to the discerning. Others, whose intentions are equally ne-farious but whose goals are less ambitious, stop short of attempting to create anything too sensational and rare. Their work is often accepted as genuine, but only for a time.

CHAPTER THREE

LATER CHINESE JADE

(Ming and Ch'ing Dynasties)

THE MAJORITY of jade appearing on the open market is of the Ch'ing dynasty (1644–1911), or even of later date. It was during Ch'ing times that Chinese craftsmen developed their skills to the highest degree, and supplies of nephrite from Turkestan were augmented by Burmese jadeite. While employing what were basically traditional patterns, these were modified to suit the taste of the day—a taste that was influenced increasingly by ideas reaching China from the West.

The last Ming emperor, Ch'ung Chêng, died in 1643 and brought to a close a dynasty that had held sway since 1368. The Manchu Tartars, who had been encroaching on the country since early in the century, finally conquered the whole land, and in 1644 the first emperor of the Ch'ing dynasty, Shun Chih, ascended the throne. He was too young to reign himself, and for a few years his uncle acted as regent, but on the death of the latter in 1651, Shun Shih assumed full powers. Ten years later he died and was succeeded by his son, K'ang-hsi.

Like his father before him, the new emperor was a minor when he came to the throne, and in 1661, when this event occurred, was seven years of age. In his case, a council of four regents administered the country until he was thirteen, when he took the reins himself. For one so young he showed an astonishing mastery of public affairs, which was to stand him in good stead for the rest of his life.

During his reign of sixty years, K'ang-hsi was able to consolidate the rule of the Manchus, and his personal character earned him respect both from his own subjects and from foreigners. The latter, in the form of Jesuit missionaries of various nationalities, had been coming and going in small numbers since the sixteenth century. Not only were they responsible for introducing many Western ideas and techniques into China, but they gained for Europe much information about Chinese practices. Of these the most famous and hitherto most elusive was the method of manufacturing porcelain that was revealed in letters sent home to Paris by the Frenchman, Père d'Entrecolles in 1712 and 1722.

Emperor K'ang-hsi was notable for his keen interest in almost every aspect of affairs in his country. In particular he studied literature and science, the latter with the aid of the Jesuits. In the library as well as on the battlefield and the hunting field his prowess earned him fame, and his patronage of the arts was equally renowned. To assist him in this last capacity the missionaries were especially assiduous, and one of them, Père Ferdinand Verbiest, was responsible for much of the organisation involved in setting up a series of imperial workshops in Peking in 1680.

The workshops were for the making of all kinds of *objets d'art*, and it had even been intended to include among them one for making porcelain. This idea was, however, abandoned, possibly because of opposition from the principal manufactory at Ching-tê Chen, which had suffered badly in a rising led by the self-styled founder of a new dynasty. He was vanquished, tried, and executed, and the porcelain works were quickly rebuilt. Alternatively, it has been suggested that the proposal to make such wares in the palace precincts lapsed because of difficulties over the supply of fuel and other bulky requirements, or owing to the risk of fire due to the proximity of the kilns to other buildings.

The workshops actually put into operation are estimated variously to have totalled twenty-seven or thirty in number, and their output included optical instruments and watches, armour, printing type, enamels, carved ivories and, not least, jade. To staff the different departments, which were housed within the walls of the Forbidden City, craftsmen specialising in each of the required skills were brought from various parts of the country. The whole project was administered by the *Kung Pu,* the official Board of Works.[1]

Although it is known that there was an atelier devoted specifically to work in jade, gold, and filigree, there is no evidence of what the employees produced. In fact, so far as the lengthy reign of K'ang-hsi is concerned there is a general ignorance of the types of jade then in favour. Owing to the disturbed state of East Turkestan and a consequent disruption of supplies of the stone, a conclusion might be drawn that very little jade was being worked at the time.

This state of affairs would seem to be borne out by the remarkably few jade objects found in two seventeenth century tombs opened in recent years. That of the Ming emperor Wan-li, who died in 1620, revealed quantities of gold, silk, and porcelain, but the jade was "disappointing in respect of both quantity and character."[2] The furnishings of the tomb of such an important personage undoubtedly called for the utmost lavishness, so that perhaps it may be assumed that either the material or the carvers, or both, were not available at the time.

The other excavation, also near Peking, was carried out in 1962, five years later than the preceding one, and a variety of jade was brought to light. Although the quantity was greater than in the Wan-li tomb, the pieces are of historical rather than of artistic importance. Nevertheless, they possibly convey some idea of what was being made at the time. In this instance the interment took place nearly sixty years after that of Wan-li, so a direct comparison is not possible. The site was the burial place of members of the family of Songgotu, a Manchu statesman who was prominent during the first half of K'ang-hsi's reign, so that the finds represent articles available at the time. Surprisingly, one tomb in particular was undisturbed and therefore had had nothing added to, or subtracted from its contents. While some, or perhaps most, of the articles had been made shortly prior to the interment, exactly how long before the event is a matter for conjecture. The jade was found with the remains of Songgotu's seven-year-old daughter who died in 1676, and included clothing ornaments, a water dropper, a cup and cover, a brush washer, and several seals, as well as some small figures of animals.

Dating of the excavated articles apparently embraces several centuries, for a report on them printed in the Peking journal *Wên-wu* in 1963 states that one was a *pi* which, the writer adds rather vaguely, is "of archaic appearance, possibly of Warring States date." In addition to those pieces mentioned above, half-a-dozen others[3] were reproduced in the pages of *Wên-wu,* but the illustrations are too indistinct to permit anything other than a superficial judgement of what they portray. Two ornaments are intricately carved, one in dark green stone with two formal dragons, and the other in white stone with an intertwining pattern. The water dropper resembles a covered winepot with a stumpy spout, and is very similar in appearance to a European teapot. This is hardly surprising since the latter in its turn was based on the design of a winepot. The cup has a ring handle, while the cover has a central button and three raised figures of lions round its edge, a motif that forms feet when the cover is removed and inverted. Seated figures of a deer and a lion form the remainder of the illustrations. The latter are in jade of a light green colour, while the water dropper and the cup and cover are recorded as being white jade. All of these pieces show a fluidity in their design which is absent from early specimens, and it is precisely this fluid quality in the design that is such a prominent feature of datable eighteenth-century jade. Such a change in appearance can be ascribed to at least two reasons: advances in lapidary technique and a change in taste on the part of buyers.

At present there is all too little evidence on which to base opinions about what may or may not have been produced during the reign of the K'ang-hsi emperor or that of his successor Yung-chêng (1723–35). The next emperor—the illustrious Ch'ien-lung—occupied the throne of China for sixty years, and personally ensured that a proportion of the finer productions of his time were marked with the year of manufacture.

Not long after he had begun to reign, Ch'ien-lung ordered his troops into East Turkestan, where there had been unrest for a considerable period. From 1750 onward, a bitter war was waged, and finally the whole terrain was conquered and named Sinkiang (New Dominion). A century or so later, in 1884, it became a province of China. From 1762, the captured country was under military rule and heavily garrisoned, so that, incidentally, the production of jade could proceed more happily than hitherto. Careful supervision of the stone gatherers was organised by Chinese officials who ceaselessly watched the operations and collected the stone for transmission to China under imperial escort.

The foregoing remarks apply to nephrite from Khotan and Yarkand, but jadeite from Burma was also coming into the country. Together with the increased supplies of nephrite, the addition of the new source ensured that there was an ample quantity of material of all types on which the jade carvers could work, and with which they could supply finished pieces for the market. The latter was led by the emperor, who avidly took for his palace any piece considered worthy of the imperial attention. Once in his ownership, many of the examples became the object of another of the royal passions—poetry. The emperor would pen lines he considered appropriate to the piece, and they would then be engraved on it. The inscriptions were carefully cut in close imitation of the imperial calligraphy and then gilded, so that to Western collectors the Oriental script enhances the appearance and interest of an object. At the same time it increases its monetary value. Such embellishment provides incontrovertible proof of what appealed to the emperor and, except when he eulogised older work, provides an indication of what was made during his reign.

The verses themselves are possibly less appealing to present-day taste than to that current when they were written. Both sentiment and language are dated, and translation from Orient to Occident only seldom bridges the gaps in time and space with success. Typical of such lines are those engraved on a libation cup, of which the exterior is carved with figures in a mountainous landscape. The emperor observed the shape of the piece and then reminisced as follows:

> This piece of jade is like a rhinoceros horn;
> It has been carved into a cup to imitate it clearly.
> There's the Leng-chia Buddhist monastery on the top of the hill
> Where I wrote some verses in the past.

Similarly, after seeing a jade plaque carved with the Taoist Paradise peopled by sages playing checkers and immersed in more studious pursuits, he wrote:

> There is great pleasure in playing chess and looking at paintings;
> It is of no moment that one's hair is white so long as one's eyes are strong.
> It is not certain that the painting is that of Sung nien;
> Nevertheless I envy anyone who looks at the Jade Plaque.[4]

In addition to having his mental impressions engraved indelibly on this or that piece of jade, the emperor often added the date on which the lines were composed. In many instances this event took place reasonably soon after the specimen was carved, but it was not uncommon for an ancient and important work of art to be treated similarly. Thus, jades bearing commendatory lines of this kind can certainly be stated to be at least as old as the reign of Ch'ien-lung, and in some cases are of very much greater antiquity.

Although, as has been mentioned above, the carvings executed during the eighteenth century exhibit a noticeable flow in their pattern when compared with earlier examples, their basic designs were often little or no different from those popular in the past. In part this was due to the innate conservatism of taste characteristic of the Chinese people, but in addition the conquest of the country by the Manchus played a role in encouraging this tendency.

Lacking any profound artistic and literary traditions of their own, the conquerors adopted those of the cultured inhabitants, and "the Manchu princes and courtiers became more Chinese than the Chinese themselves."[5] The latter, saddened and buffeted by conflict, resigned themselves to Manchu overlordship and turned back to their historic past which seemed to them, in contrast to the present, to have been a golden age of freedom, progress, and cultural beauty. The Manchus were well aware of the artistic achievements of the Chinese in former days, and not only grew to respect these attainments but to encourage their study and imitation. Thus, from the reign of K'ang-hsi onwards there was a continual and expanding interest in classical China: in the art forms of the T'ang and Sung dynasties of some five hundred to a thousand years earlier.

At the great porcelain manufactory at Ching-tê Chen much time was spent in reproducing the various forms made in the past. Equal effort was directed to imitating old glazes, the secret of whose composition had in some cases long ago been lost. The most renowned director general of the imperial factory during the eighteenth century was T'ang Ying, who was appointed to the post in the year that saw Ch'ien-lung ascend the throne, 1735. Of him it was recorded that "his close copies of famous wares of the past were without exception worthy partners [of the originals]; his copies of every kind of well-known glaze were without exception cleverly matched."[6] Imitating was not confined to early examples in the same material, but extended to a wide range of what may be thought unsuitable models. In this connexion the author of the *T'ao Shuo* noted in 1774 that "among all works of art in carved gold and embossed silver, chiselled stone, lacquer, mother-of-pearl, bamboo and wood, gourd, and shell there is not one that is not now reproduced in porcelain."

Collectors and students of eighteenth-century porcelain will have seen or read about extant specimens that confirm the foregoing comments. While it is not usually a matter of any difficulty to detect a piece of chinaware simulating lacquer or one of the other materials mentioned, later copies of early forms and glazes can often inspire debate. Further, the potters of the time not only imitated the appearance—the shape and colouring—of early work, but frequently added marks counterfeiting those on the originals. Admiration and emulation could go no farther.

Similarly, copies in jade of early jades were made throughout the Ch'ing dynasty, both during the eighteenth and the nineteenth centuries, but many new shapes were introduced and fresh combinations of old decorative motifs were applied to them. The mixture of old and new can be treacherous to modern eyes, but a study of the details of doubtful examples will usually determine their true age—or youth. Further, it must be remembered that jadeite, the colourful stone from Burma, did not reach China until towards the end of the eighteenth century, therefore carvings in it cannot predate that time.

A conspicuous feature of much of the Ch'ing jade is the large size of examples when compared with those of earlier date. While many pieces, perhaps more often than is generally admitted, are no older than the late nineteenth century, a proportion were carved in the reign of Ch'ien-lung. The preponderance of big pieces resulted from better organisation at the mines, as well as a number of other factors, including demand for the stone and improvements in methods of carving. The craftsmen were able to do much more intricate work at greater speed, and while the perfection of finish they attained is not to every taste, it is a tribute to their craftsmanship and patience. The vessels made from jade in the past were famous because of their rarity and were extolled as examples to be followed, with the result that from the time of K'ang-hsi onward every endeavour was made to imitate them to the point of deception; or, alternatively, to surpass them.

The most typical of mid- to late-eighteenth-century pieces of jade are the "boulder" carvings: roughly shaped lumps of the stone worked with scenes in low relief. Probably the largest of them is the example in Peking bearing scenes showing the legendary flood-prevention works of the equally legendary Yü, who is supposed to have lived about 2300 B.C.—a date that varies from one authority to another. The father of Yü, the emperor Yau, was unable to deal with the disastrous overflowing of a river, perhaps the Yellow River. After nine years Yü was able to drain away the inundations by cutting canals through hills and, in the opinion of a modern critic, Baron Ferdinand von Richthofen (1833–1905), "performed feats of engineering compared to which the construction of the St. Gotthard Tunnel in Switzerland, without blasting, would be child's play."

Other boulder carvings are of a more reasonable size, but also depict scenes that are part of Chinese legend. One popular subject is the Islands of the Blest, supposedly situated off the coast of Kiangsu and inhabited by fairies or immortals or by both, who lived by eating gemstones found on the seashore and by drinking the wine which flowed from a jade rock. The islands also produced the *ling chih*, the plant of immortality, a fungus revered as the emblem of longevity and conferring eternal life if it was found and eaten. The story of such a never-never land is paralleled in many other countries, and is one that appeals to all men. Certainly Ch'ien-lung was attracted to it, for a number of boulders bearing his poetic thoughts are recorded.

The *ling chih* was the basis of the *ju-i,* or sceptre, also a symbol of longevity, and sometimes made wholly or partly of jade. A ceremonial object, it was sometimes given as a present—one was bestowed on Lord Macartney, head of an embassy from Great Britain, when he was on an official mission to Peking in the late eighteenth century. The *ju-i* is usually about thirty centimetres in length with one end curved upward and swelling into a shaped plaque, the latter sometimes carved with bats (for happiness), bamboo (for long life), and other appropriate emblems.

Another carving, perhaps less often seen, is also symbolic. The inedible citron, *Citrus medica,* has a number of slender fingerlike projections and has been given the name *fo shou,* or Buddha's-Hand citron. Its religious connexion stems from its shape which is reminiscent of one of the classic positions of the hand of Buddha in which the little finger and the index finger point upwards. The actual fruit has a powerful fragrance and, besides its religious significance, is also emblematic of wealth because it is seen to resemble a hand grasping money. In jade the citron has been carved either laid on its side as an ornament, or as an upright vase.

Another vase form consists of the three trees—pine, plum, and bamboo—although these are more generally found carved in relief as ornament. All three are plentiful in most parts of China and, being hardy plants, have come to symbolise longevity.

Buddhism has inspired many of the human figures carved in jade, although these are comparatively scarce. One of the forms more frequently met with, is the goddess Kuan-yin, the most popular of the female deities in China. The slender, often sinuous and always graceful form of Kuan-yin holding a child in her arms has been much admired even outside the confines of China, possibly because of the superficial likeness to the Virgin and Child of Christianity. Few such figures are of great age, and the tall examples averaging about thirty centimetres in height, in well-coloured jadeite, are mostly products of the past half-century. Many of them are mounted on metal bases and, with appropriate fittings, make decorative, if costly, table lamps.

Two of the eighteen followers (*lohan,* or *arhat*) of Buddha, are shown in Plates 63 and 64. Each of the *lohan* is credited with supernatural powers and each has a personal retinue of between five hundred and a thousand subordinates. The two depicted are Nagasena—reputed to be adept at propounding the essentials of Buddhism and also to have had a commanding presence and wit—and his companion Vanavasa, invariably shown seated in meditation with closed eyes; in the present instance he is holding an incense burner in one hand and a ritual object in the other.

Eight of the *lohan* are seen on a table screen illustrated in Plate 66. They are seated on a mountain or beside a river which divides one of their number from the others; a few gnarled trees are growing and clouds stretch across the top of the scene. Screens of this kind were made for a number of uses, some being intended for the family altar and others fulfilling a purely decorative purpose.

While bowls of small size were made as early as 200 B.C., those with a diameter of twenty-five to thirty centimetres, demanding selected material and great perseverance in working it, came from the hands of carvers from the late eighteenth century onward. Generally no more than five to eight centimetres in depth, they usually have a pair of handles and in some instances are carved in the interior as well as on the outside of the body. Again, emblems of happiness, long life, and other good omens are featured, and the handles often take the form of monster masks (*t'ao t'ieh*), with loose rings hanging from their mouths. Not only did the making of such bowls require a sizeable and perfect piece of jade, but the process of hollowing the inside was complicated, and unless carefully executed could end in disaster. The portion to be removed was scored with a series of parallel cuts at right angles, and the standing fragments were then knocked away. The cavity thus produced was only approximate, and had then to be subjected to a long period of grinding in order to reduce it to the required shape and smoothness.

The period saw the making of many types of containers, from the three-legged, covered incense burners to tall quadrangular vases, most of which owed their origin to bronzes of earlier date. Decoration on all of them was mostly in relief, but in some instances was incised and gilded. The more elaborate vases were given loose ring handles, and some had the cover attached to the body by a chain; the entire article, vase, cover, and links, being carved from a single piece of jade. Needless to say, the production of all these pieces was not confined to Ch'ien-lung's reign, but continued well into the nineteenth century, and indeed still goes on.

The variety of animals, fishes, and birds that were carved in jade grew wider as the Ch'ing dynasty progressed. Both real and legendary animals and their monster counterparts abound among the jades of the period, with the monsters predominating. Among these the Dog of Fo, a lionlike creature to be seen in stone outside various Buddhist temples, and familiar to the china collector from the many examples in porcelain with *famille verte* and *famille rose* decoration, rears its head. A conventionalised lion, it is sacred to Buddha and, as in the West, its leonine character is a symbol of valour and energy. The usual posture is seated (sejant), with a curled mane and a trifid tail; and the female of the species is generally accompanied by a cub. The male, in similar posture, rests one of his paws on a ball. This is an allusion to the Chinese legend that lions produced milk from their paws—country people, it is said, used to leave suitable globelike receptacles lying around in hilly country so that roving lions, all unsuspecting, might play with them and in consequence fill them with milk. Lions were not indigenous to China, and knowledge of them in the flesh was probably confined to the court at certain times when gifts of the beasts were made to the emperor.

Often confused with the Dog of Fo is the *kylin,* or *ch'i-lin.* Although resembling each other slightly in appearance they are in fact quite different. The *kylin* is a male and female composite not based on any one living animal, and in addition to having a lengthy history in Chinese writings, is said to have lived to the ripe age of ten thousand years. It is depicted with the head of a dragon, deer's hoofs, shoulders aflame, and a bushy tail. As one of the Four Supernatural Creatures, it is representative of Perfect Good and Married Bliss. According to the *Ku yü t'u p'u,* a carved *kylin* was discovered in the grave of a man buried in about 2160 B.C.

A third monster which shares some of its features with the others is *lung-ma,* which has a dragon's body supported on the legs of a horse. The animal is supposed to have emerged from the Yellow River bearing on its back the eight trigrams, a series of short and long lines; or, as depicted in Plate 110, it appears with the Books of Knowledge at its side (see also p. 80).

The Yellow River makes its appearance also in the legends of fishes, in which it is related that sturgeon which fight their way upstream with success are transformed into dragons. These, however, are not known to have been carved in jade. The more commonplace carp is to be seen in the form of boxes, vases, snuff bottles, and table ornaments. Fish in general tended to be regarded in China as the repository of numerous desirable qualities and virtues such as wealth, happiness, and connubial bliss, and it was customary to make a gift of a pair of jade fishes at betrothal. Whether all of the surviving examples of such objects were made for this reason, or indeed actually given, is a matter hard to judge. As in many another case, an object used in, or connected with some ceremony became in the course of time regarded as a thing of value and a source of pleasure in itself, its former associations largely forgotten.

In the Ch'ing dynasty the habit of taking snuff spread to China, and during the course of the eighteenth century the jade snuff bottle made its appearance. The requirements of the snuff taker being for limited quantities of the powder, the containers could be quite small—a fact that ideally suited jade for the purpose. Specially chosen pieces were often used, and snuff bottles were made in the rarest colours. Every technique of the carver was exploited to make these small objects of the finest workmanship and design, the ingenuity of the carver stretched to its limit in the use of the "skin" of the jade pebble as part of the design. Really exceptional specimens were carved from stone displaying more than one colour, the effect resembling that of shell cameos. The double or multiple colour effect was imitated in Peking opaque glass, sometimes with deceptive fidelity.

Laufer wrote that "in ancient China, jade took also the place of valuable money, and was occasionally also turned into coinage," and he illustrated an example. The latter resembles a blank Yale key and has characters inscribed on it which read "Great money, fifty." He also shows two bronze keys of the time of Wang Mang the Usurper (A.D. 8–23), which are of similar shape but with a cen-

LATER CHINESE JADE
Plates 52–130

52. Seated horse. Ming dynasty.
Length, 31.7 cm; weight, 28 lbs.
Somerset de Chair, Essex, England.

53. *Recumbent water buffalo. Dark green. Ming dynasty. Length, 40.6 cm. Metropolitan Museum of Art, New York. Gift of Mrs. Edward S. Harkness, 1936.*

54. *Underside of seated horse in Plate 52.*

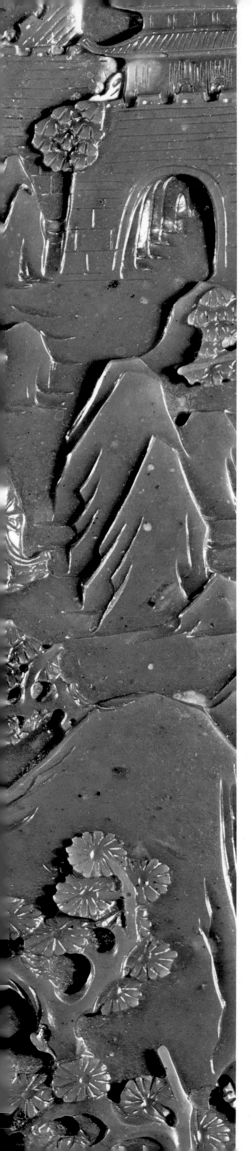

55–56. *Detail and full view of table screen depicting the meeting between Lao Tsu, founder of the Taoist school of philosophy, represented riding in a bullock cart accompanied by a child attendant, and Yun Hi, governor of the Han-kuh frontier pass. The reverse is incised with peaches of longevity, bats of happiness, and floral scrolls. Eighteenth century. 33 × 25.4 cm. The screen came from the Yüan Ming Yüan, Peking, in 1860. Christie's, London.*

57. Boulder carved with a figure holding a paddle and standing on the steps of a grotto, while on the left a boat emerges from a cavern. Above are trees on a hillside, and over all are clouds. An inscription on the back records that the carving was done to the order of Ch'ien-lung in the spring of 1748. Dark green. Height, 38 cm. (without stand); length, 58.5 cm. Christie's, London.

58. Small boulder, light green, carved with a waterfall, and a tree growing on a mountain. A sage points upwards. The inscription, probably composed by Ch'ien-lung, reads:

Jadelike glass curtains, crystal screen,
Exquisite to observe and to hear.
Leaning on a bamboo staff, a hermit can pass a moment
And feel he is knocking at the gates of the clouds as he
emerges from his hut.

Ch'ien-lung period. Height, 19.7 cm. Seattle Art Museum. Eugene Fuller Memorial Collection.

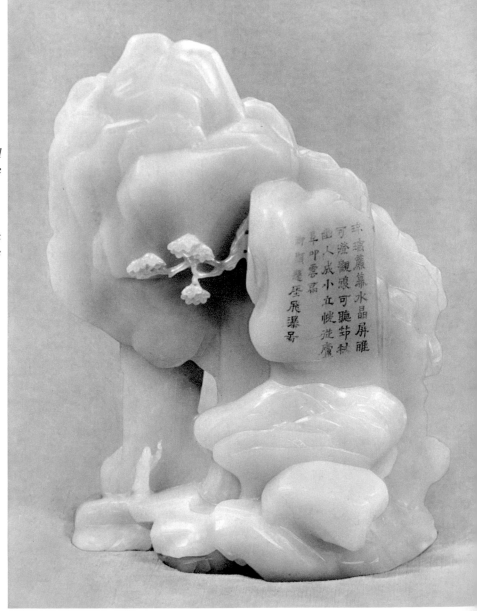

59. Boulder carved in high relief with two horses, one drinking from a stream, and ▷ with pine trees on a hillside. Dark celadon colour. Early Ch'ing dynasty. Height, 30.5 cm. Spink & Son, London.

60. *The lohan Panthaka painted in gold on a jade tablet mounted in a brocade border. Late eighteenth century. 22.2 × 13.6 cm. This is one of the leaves of a book illustrating and describing the original sixteen Buddhist lohans. Chester Beatty Library, Dublin.*

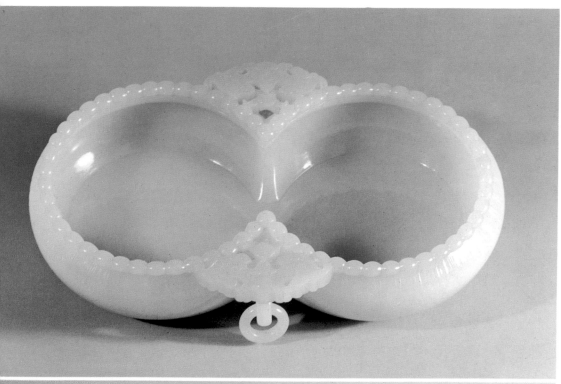

61. Double bowl with beaded rims, the conventionalised-bat handles holding loose rings. Ch'ien-lung period. Length, 22.2 cm. Victoria & Albert Museum, London.

62. Bowl carved with two carp. Ch'ien-lung period. Diameter, 21.1 cm. Victoria & Albert Museum, London.

65. *Vase in the form of a fou shou, or Buddha's-hand citron. Light green to white. Ch'ien-lung period. Height, 16.2 cm. Metropolitan Museum of Art, New York. Gift of Heber R. Bishop, 1902.*

63–64. *Two lohans. Plate 63: Fa-na-p'o-ssu, or Vanavasa, meditating with downcast eyes. Olive green. Ch'ien-lung period. Height, 24.1 cm. Plate 64: Na-ka-hsi-na, or Naga-sena, a lohan possessed of a ready wit and commanding presence. Pale olive green. Ch'ien-lung period. Height, 24.1 cm. Both figures from Spink & Son, London.*

66. *Inscribed table screen carved with figures of lohans.* ▷ *Dark green. Eighteenth century. 34.2 × 22.9 cm. Spink & Son, London.*

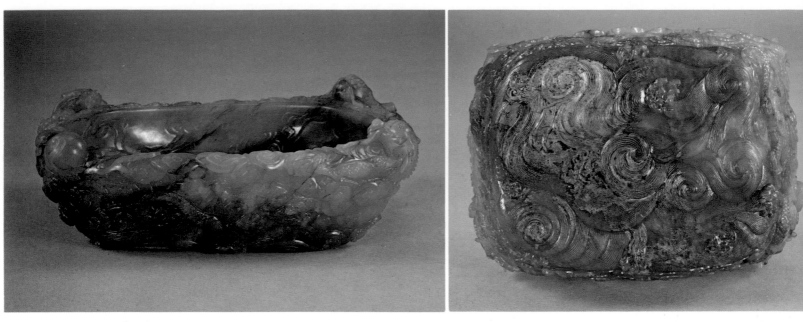

67–68. *Two views of a bowl carved on the exterior with clouds from which emerge three dragons chasing a pearl. The interior is carved with clouds, and the exterior of the bottom with whirlpools. Late Ming. Length, 15.6 cm. City Hall Museum, Hong Kong.*

70. *Bowl with four* ling-chih, *or fungus-pattern, feet, and two lion's-head mask handles with loose rings suspended from them. The base has an incised four-character mark of Ch'ien-lung. Diameter, 20.5 cm. Christie's, London.*

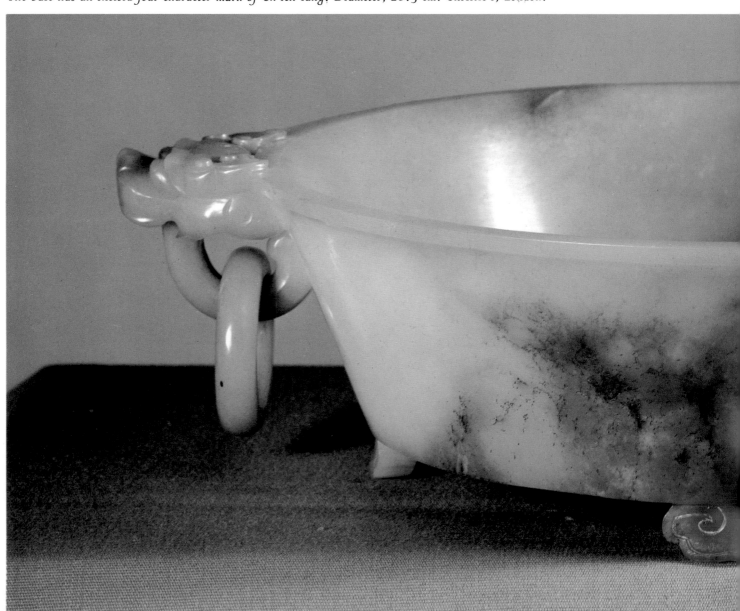

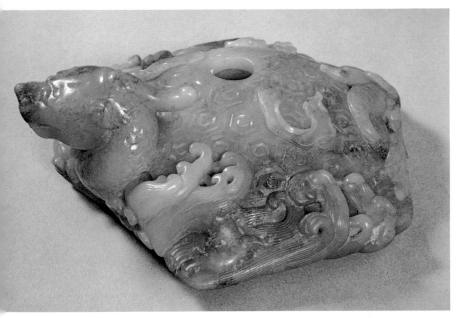

69. *Waterpot for a scholar's desk in the form of a dragon-headed turtle in a whirlpool. The waves surround the creature and continue on the underside. Late Ming. Length, 17 cm. City Hall Museum, Hong Kong.*

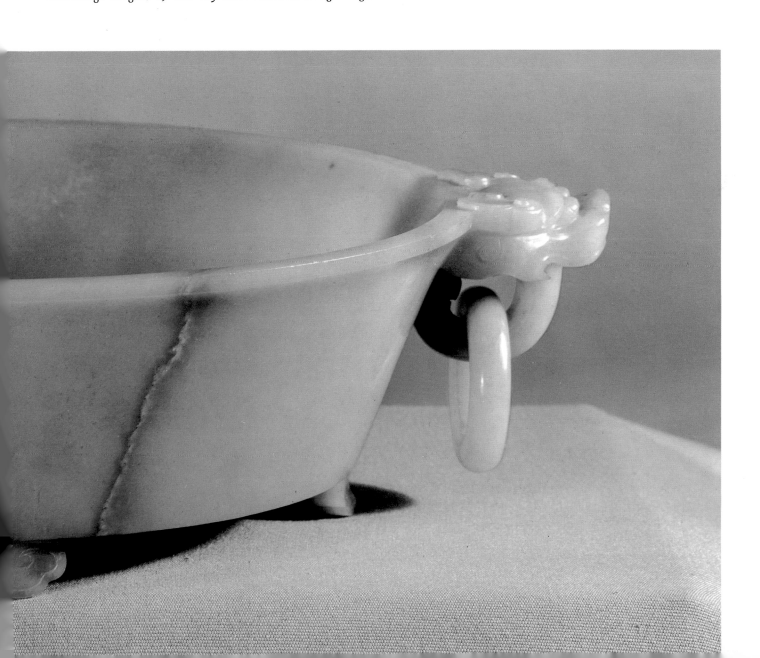

71. *Bowl and cover, eight-lobed. The flat rim is carved with four butterflies between* ling-chih *fungus patterns. Loops under the latter hold four loose rings. The knob is flower capped. Translucent white. Ch'ien-lung period. Diameter, 16.5 cm. Spink & Son, London.*

72. *Bowl carved in panels with a pattern of peony flowers and leaves. Mottled sage green. K'ang-hsi period. Width, 12.7 cm. Christie's, London.*

73. *Bowl with handles in the shape of dragons' heads with loose rings, and feet in the form of stylised* ling-chih. *The interior and exterior are decorated with sprays of flowers in gold lacquer with brown pencilling. Translucent greenish white. Square seal mark of Ch'ien-lung. Width, 22.2 cm. Spink & Son, London.*

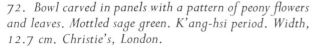

75–76 *(overleaf). Two views of table screen. White, inlaid with green jade, brown agate, pink crystal, lapis lazuli, and other gemstones. The green jade frame is inlaid with pink coral. Eighteenth century. Screen 25.3 × 19.7 cm. Overall height, 41.9 cm. Spink & Son, London.*

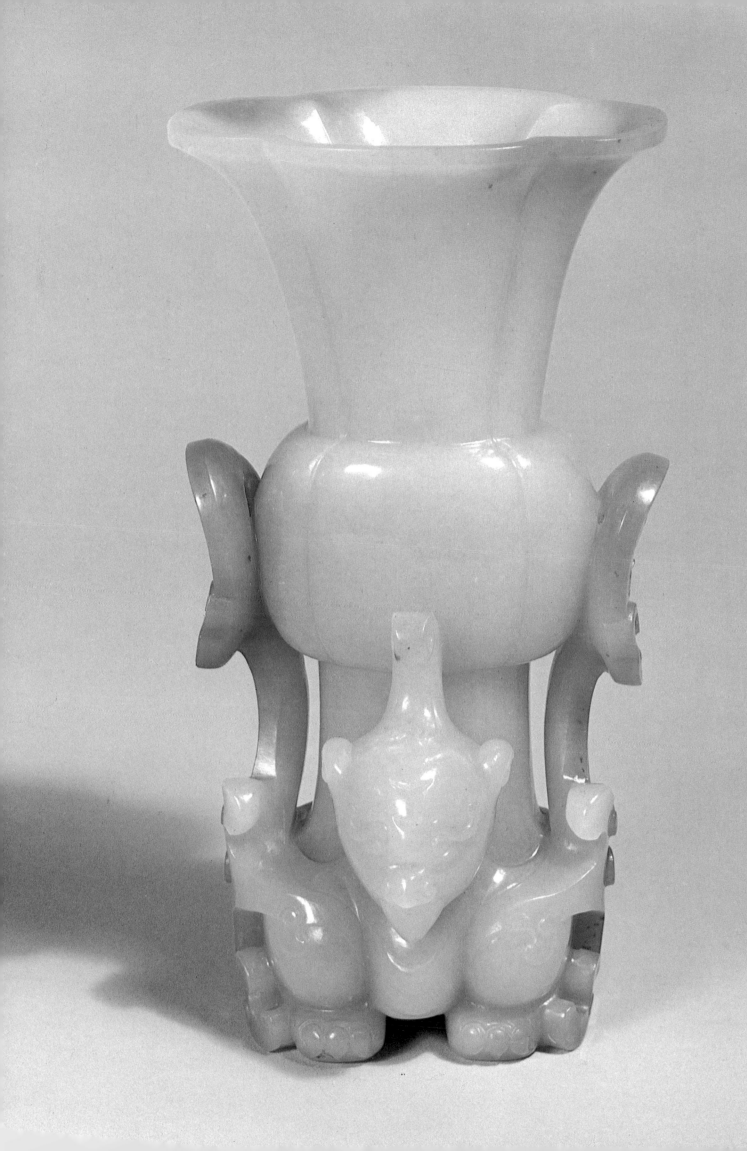

77. *Seated buffalo. Ming dynasty. Length, 32.4 cm. Somerset de Chair, Essex, England.*

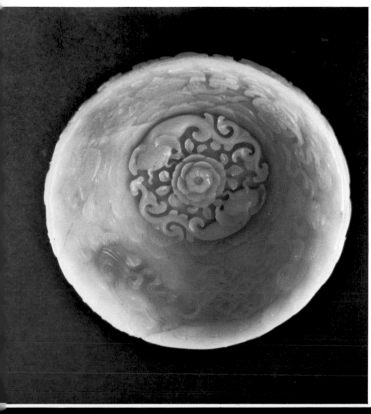

78. Oval bowl, probably a brush washer, carved with four dragons round the exterior. Ming dynasty. Width, 13 cm. National Palace Museum, Taipei.

79–80. Bottom and side views of bowl carved with dragons amid clouds. Ming dynasty. Diameter, 15.5 cm. National Palace Museum, Taipei.

81. *Bowl with handles and interior carved with hibiscus and peonies. Spinach green.
Ch'ien-lung period. Width, 30.5 cm. Christie's, London.*

82. *Bowl carved on the exterior with twelve magpies perched on blossoming plum
branches. The handles have loose rings. Whitish colour. Ch'ien-lung period. Width,
23.5 cm. Sotheby's, London.*

83. *Vase and cover joined by a chain, the whole
carved from a single piece of stone. The decoration
is a phoenix and a tree, and the cover is surmounted
by a ch'i-lin. Translucent whitish colour. Chia-
ch'ing period. Height, 31.4 cm. Formerly in the
collection of G. F. Farrow.*

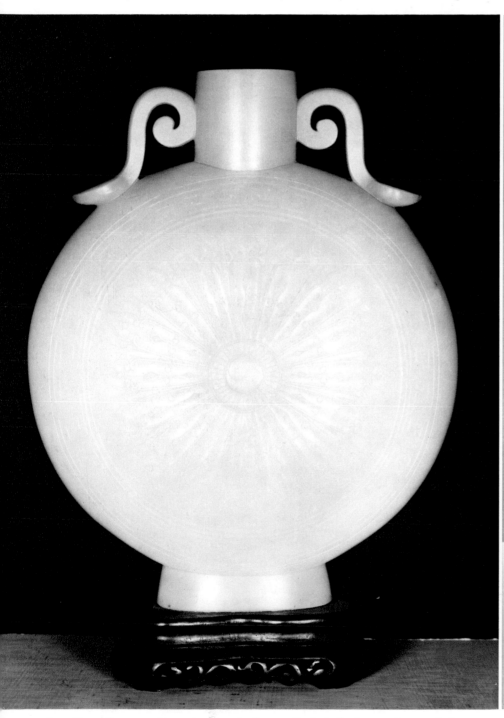

84. *Vase of green-white jade shaped after a pilgrim's flask, sometimes called a moon flask. Early Ch'ing dynasty. Height, 21.6 cm. The shallow carving on either side centres on a yin-yang symbol. Formerly in the collection of G. F. Farrow.*

85. *Vase and cover carved with figures and pavilions in a mountainous landscape. The handles are winged phoenix heads with loose rings, while the finial is a dragon. White. Ch'ing dynasty. Height, 45 cm. Metropolitan Museum of Art, New York. Bequest of Jacob Ruppert, 1939.*

88. *Vase carved with two bands of carp, ducks, and tortoises symbolical ▷ of life in the water, in the air, and on land. The handles are dragons' heads with loose rings. On the base an inscription reads: "Made in the Ch'ien-lung period in the style of the antique." Pale translucent celadon colour. Ch'ien-lung period. Height, 43.2 cm. Formerly the vase was in the collection of Admiral Humman, commander-in-chief of the French naval forces in China in the late nineteenth century. Spink & Son, London. (See page 93 for detail.)*

86. Tsun *in the shape of a* ch'i-lin *monster bearing a vase on its back. Loose ring handles. Ch'ing dynasty. Height, 22.1 cm. National Palace Museum, Taipei.*

87. *Vase in the form of two leaping carp. Ch'ing dynasty. Height, 11.5 cm. National Palace Museum, Taipei.*

89. *Snuff bottle carved with monkeys in a grotto. Ch'ing dynasty. Height, 8.1 cm. Private collection. (See Plate 3 for detail.)*

90. *Snuff bottle carved with figures in a landscape, the reverse with an inscription, signatures, and seals. Collection of Hugh M. Moss. (See Plate 1 for detail.)*

91. *Snuff bottle of unusually brilliantly coloured jadeite.*

92. *Snuff bottle carved with a sage in a landscape. Ch'ing dynasty. Height, 6.1 cm. Collection of Hugh M. Moss. (See Plate 4 for detail.)*

93. *Snuff bottle of yellowish green nephrite. Ch'ing dynasty. Height, 6.9 cm. Collection of H. H. Ross.*

94. *Snuff bottle carved to simulate partial draping with cloth. Ch'ing dynasty. Height, 6.3 cm. Collection of Hugh M. Moss.*

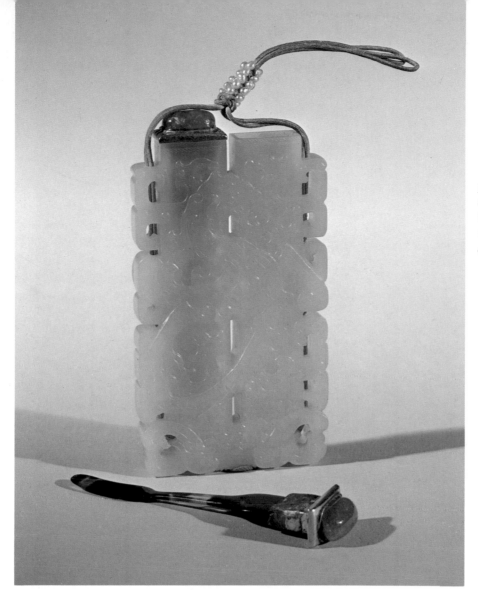

97. *Double snuff bottle, carved and pierced. Translucent white. Ch'ing dynasty. Height, 8.6 cm. Collection of E. E. Brake, London.*

95. *Snuff bottle of spinach-green nephrite. Collection of Hugh M. Moss.*

96. *Two snuff bottles formed from pebbles by removing some of the brown "skin." Ch'ing dynasty. Height (left), 5.7 cm.; (right), 6.3 cm. Collection of E. E. Brake, London.*

100. *Snuff bottle in the form of a bear and cub. White. Ch'ing dynasty. Height, 7.1 cm. Collection of Alex. S. Cussons.*

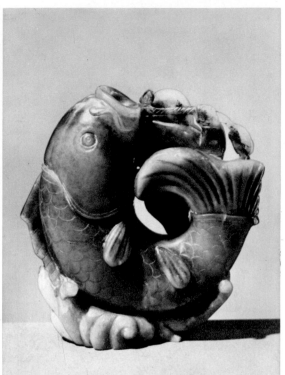

98–99. *Two views of a vase formed as a group of carp with the sage Liu-hai, who holds the string of gold coins with which he lured the three-legged toad at his feet. Dark smoky blue grey, and white misted with blue grey. Ch'ien-lung period. Height, 11.4 cm. Spink & Son, London.*

101. *Pebble carved as a horse and monkey. This early Ch'ing carving was later converted into a snuff bottle. White with traces of brown. Height, 6.9 cm. Private collection.*

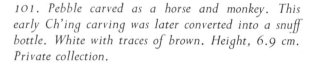

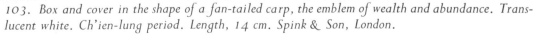

103. *Box and cover in the shape of a fan-tailed carp, the emblem of wealth and abundance. Translucent white. Ch'ien-lung period. Length, 14 cm. Spink & Son, London.*

120

104. *Elephant. Dark green and white. Ch'ien-lung period. Length, 20.3 cm. Spink & Son, London.*

102. *Waterpot carved with dragons chasing a pearl amid clouds. Green. Ch'ing dynasty. Length, 39.4 cm. Gulbenkian Museum of Oriental Art, Durham, England.*

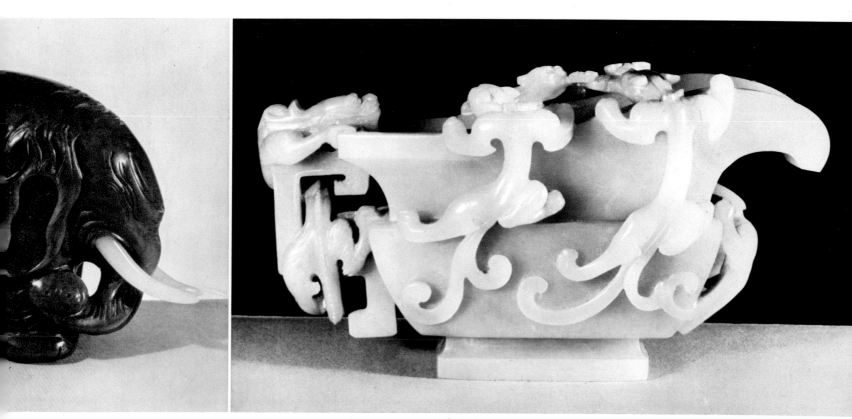

105. *Ewer carved with dragons in relief. Pale green. Ch'ien-lung period. Length, 22.8 cm. Spink & Son, London.*

106. *Smoothed pebble carved with a stylised animal. Such pieces were kept in the pocket and handled for the enjoyment of the feel of the stone. Ch'ing dynasty. Length, 10.1 cm. Collection of E. E. Brake, London.*

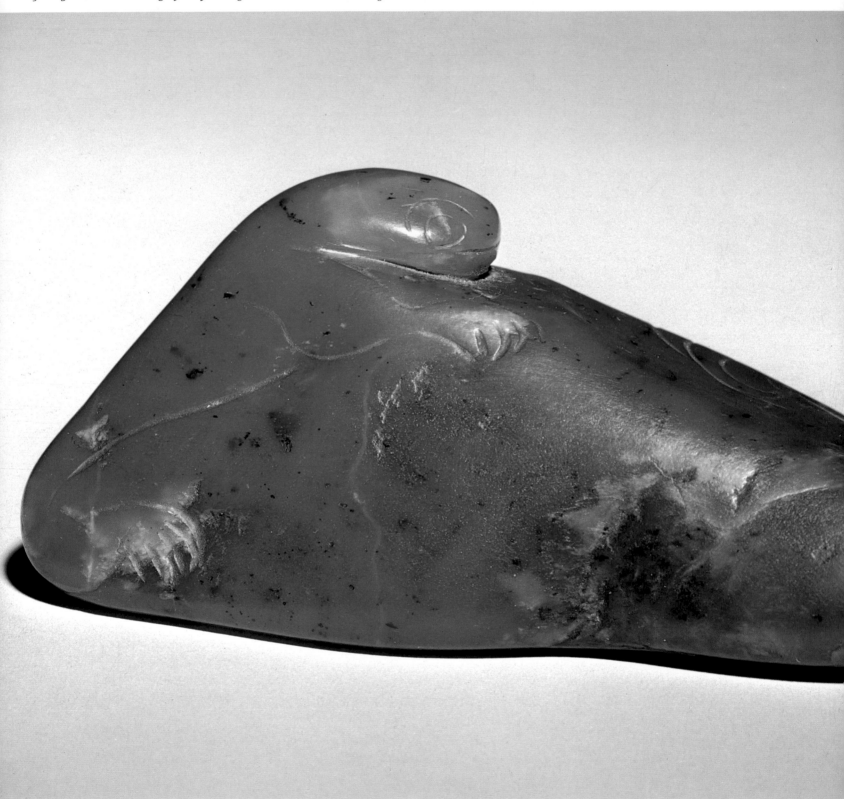

107–8. *Three views of silver-mounted box and cover with an elephant design. The extreme thinness of the jade can be seen in Plate 107. Ch'ing dynasty. Diameter, 5.1 cm. Collection of E. E. Brake, London.*

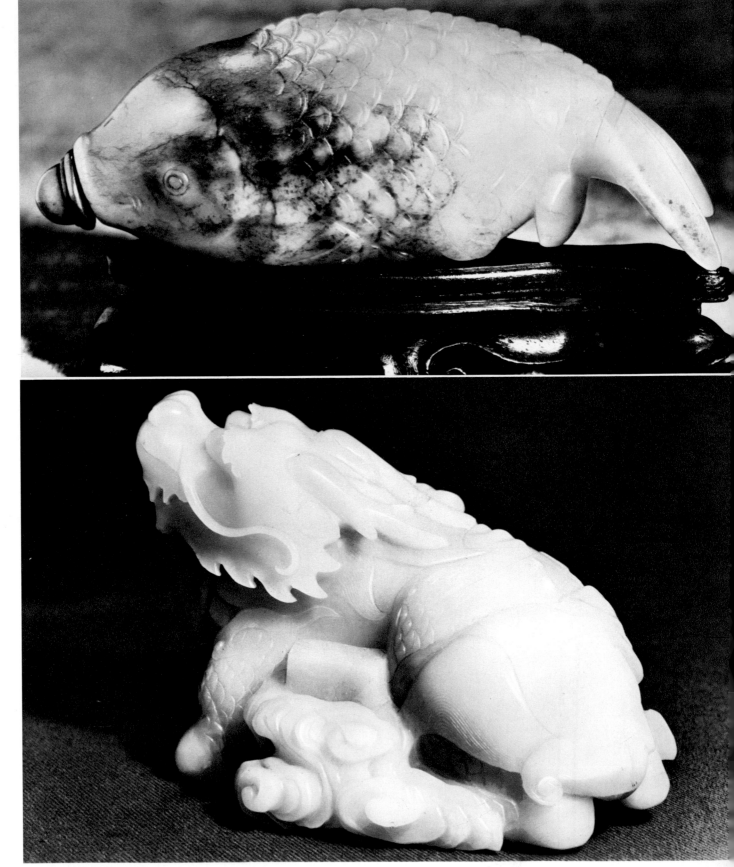

109. *Snuff bottle in the form of a fish. Greenish grey and brown. Ch'ing dynasty. Length, 7 cm. Collection of Hugh M. Moss.*

110. *Dragon-horse (lung-ma), shown rising from the Yellow River carrying the books of knowledge. Greenish white. Length, 18 cm. Fitzwilliam Museum, Cambridge, England.*

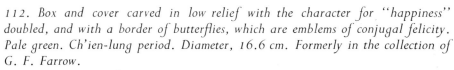

111. *Box, carved and pierced, with flying bats, flowers, and leaves. Grey-white colour. Ch'ien-lung period. Diameter, 10.5 cm. Seattle Art Museum. Eugene Fuller Memorial Collection.*

112. *Box and cover carved in low relief with the character for "happiness" doubled, and with a border of butterflies, which are emblems of conjugal felicity. Pale green. Ch'ien-lung period. Diameter, 16.6 cm. Formerly in the collection of G. F. Farrow.*

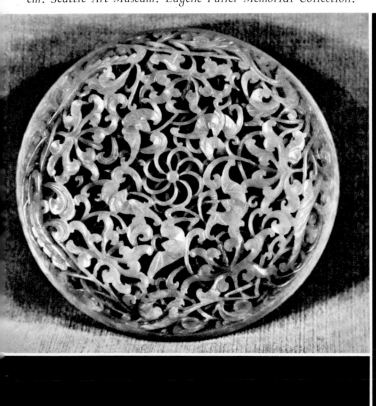

113. *Snuff bottle carved with a scene of a boat by a river bank. The inscription, filled with powder for photographing, is the third line from a poem by the T'ang poet Chang Chi. The poem is about hearing the midnight bell from a temple while in a boat near Soochow. Greenish yellow and brown. Ch'ing dynasty. Collection of Alex. S. Cussons.*

114. *Ewer carved with flowers in high relief springing from incised pairs of leaves, the scroll handle and loose ring similarly ornamented. Pale greenish white. Ch'ien-lung period. Height, 12.3 cm. Metropolitan Museum of Art, New York. Gift of Heber R. Bishop, 1902.*

115. *Figure of an attendant carrying a bowl. Spinach green with dark flecks. Late Ming or early Ch'ing dynasty. Height, 30.4 cm. Metropolitan Museum of Art, New York. Gift of Heber R. Bishop, 1902.*

116. *Bowl of quatrefoil shape containing flowers, berries, and leaves. The bowl is celadon colour, the leaves dark green, and the flowers and berries pale green, carnelian, coral, and crystal. Ch'ien-lung period. Height, 21.6 cm. Spink & Son, London.*

117. *Incense burner on tripod base, constructed in ▷ eight sections, pierced and carved with t'ao t'ieh masks, archaic dragons, and other motifs, and hung with loose rings and bells. Jadeite. Height, 77.5 cm. Square seal mark of Ch'ien-lung on the base. Parke-Bernet Galleries, New York.*

118. Dish carved as an open flower. Translucent green. Ch'ien-lung period. Diameter, 22.2 cm. Spink & Son, London.

119. **Pi.** *Carved and incised with a hexagonal basketry pattern. In each hexagon is a commalike figure. Translucent grey with a greenish cast and slate-blue clouding. Ch'ing dynasty. Diameter, 24.6 cm. Freer Gallery of Art, Washington, D.C.*

120–21. Detail and full view of brush pot carved with sages in caverns in a mountainous landscape with trees. Ch'ing dynasty. Height, 15.8 cm. National Palace Museum, Taipei.

122. Incense burner and cover carved with stylised ▷ dragons and flowers. Ch'ien-lung period. Height, 27.3 cm. Victoria & Albert Museum, London. (See frontispiece for detail.)

123. A pair of pricket candlesticks, each in the form of a duck standing on a tortoise. The duck is an emblem of felicity, the tortoise of longevity. Pale celadon colour. Ch'ien-lung period. Height to the top of the spikes, 21.6 cm. Spink & Son, London.

124. A pair of pricket candlesticks with bell-shaped bases, carved in low relief with auspicious emblems and scrolling foliage. The stands are of contemporary gilt bronze decorated with bands of cloisonné enamel. Dark green. Ch'ien-lung period. Height to the top of the spikes, 41.9 cm. Spink & Son, London.

125. *Altar set comprising an incense burner and cover carved with stylised dragons and surmounted by two Buddhist lions with a ball, and a pair of vases similarly carved, with dragons'-head fittings from which hang loose rings. Translucent white ("melting snow") with splashes of emerald green. Heights: incense burner, 34.3 cm.; vases, 33.7 cm. Spink & Son, London.*

127. *Incense burner carved and pierced with the eight emblems of happy augury (pa chi hsiang). The cover is hung with six engraved gold bells while the body is carved in low relief with dragons and phoenixes, and raised on three dragon-headed feet. Translucent white. Ch'ien-lung period. Height, 31.1 cm. From the Summer Palace, Peking. Spink & Son, London.*

128. *Wine ewer carved with the eight emblems of happy augury. The spout springs from a dragon's head, and the knob of the cover is carved and pierced in the form of a dragon. Translucent seaweed green. Four-character mark of Ch'ien-lung. Height, 40 cm. Spink & Son, London.*

129. *Cap stand removed from the throne room of the Summer Palace during the Boxer Rebellion, 1900. The stand is inlaid with butterflies among carved gourds and leaves. The stem has loose rings, and a balustrade surrounds the base. The contemporary rosewood base, on which it rests, is inlaid with silver and has small pillars of gilt bronze. Translucent green, and white. Ch'ien-lung period. Height overall, 33 cm. Spink & Son, London.*

130 (Overleaf). *Title page of* A Discussion on the Carriage with a League-Recording Drum, *engraved and gilded in imitation of* ▷ *the Ch'ien-lung emperor's handwriting, 1778. Grey green. One of four panels, each 20.6 × 10.5 cm. Chester Beatty Library, Dublin.*

御製記里鼓車說

tral square hole in place of the circular one in the bow of the jade example. Other jade coins are recorded, but it is most improbable that they were ever in circulation as normal currency. Doubtless they were produced for the edification of numismatists and collectors of jade, and probably few of them, if any, predate the nineteenth century.

There are numerous ancient records of incribed jade tablets whose purpose was to enshrine for posterity the great thoughts of great men—and even some of their more prosaic sentiments. The durability of jade was obviously ideal for the purpose, but the carelessness and destructiveness of humanity has caused most of the tablets to vanish. Surviving examples are thin plaques, carefully engraved with the incisions often gilded, while those carrying illustrations were also silvered, and sometimes heightened with colour. Yet others were treated in the manner of conventional paper or board, the texts painted or applied in gold leaf over a varnish.

Inscribed jade tablets were employed for imperial sacrificial ceremonies, and by the time of the emperor T'ai Tsung (A.D. 627–49) they were considered to be indispensable for the practice. In the year 1008 the emperor Chên Tsung made a ritual offering of two boxes containing seventeen inscribed jade slabs on the summit of Mount T'ai, a 1525-metre-high object of veneration over many centuries. They were found in 1747, when Ch'ien-lung had been on the throne for a little more than a decade, but would seem to have disappeared subsequently.

Such ceremonial tablets bore a single vertical line of characters, but by the mid-seventeenth century each carried several lines and resembled in appearance the pages of a conventional book. This likeness extended to binding the jades together by means of silver wire, strong cords, or thongs, and giving them protective covers of carved wood.

No fewer than fifteen jade books are in the Chester Beatty Library in Dublin,[7] of which the earliest example is dated 1648. Another records a poem written by Ch'ien-lung on the subject of the immense jade bowl in Peking, which is described at length by Professor Hansford.[8] The bowl probably dates from the thirteenth or fourteenth century and was almost certainly seen and recorded by the traveller Friar Odoric of Pordenone, who wrote that it was mounted in gold with "fringes of network of great pearls hanging therefrom." Lacking its previous embellishments, it was discovered, so the story goes, by the emperor Ch'ien-lung, who purchased it from some Taoist priests in whose ownership it had served for storing vegetables. He cast the story into Chinese verse, had it inscribed on the bowl, and also in the form of a jade book which is now in Dublin.

To European eyes perhaps the most attractive of the extant books is one depicting each of the original sixteen *lohan,* a group of Buddha's disciples to whose ranks were added two further members in comparatively recent times. Among them is Panthaka, known also as Pantha the Elder and as Pan-t'o-ka, one of the greatest of the disciples. In the accompanying text he is described in the following words: "He understands the whole of the Law and impeaches or justifies the scriptures. Around him waters flow, the rocks are cold, the wind passes, flowers are fragrant. He proclaims the glorious holy scripture to the whole universe. He sweeps all prejudice away. Of him it may be truly said that he has seen the futility of the senses and the intellect."[9]

It is appropriate that the features and description of one who "by thought aimed at excellence" should be recorded in that most perfect and enduring of natural substances—jade.

PART TWO

OTHER EASTERN JADE

CHAPTER FOUR

ISLAMIC JADE

ONE OF the many long-standing arguments concerning jade is whether nephrite was carved in the East other than in China. The material itself was familiar in Central Asia from at least 1426, the year in which Ulugh Beg erected in Samarkand a tomb of jade in memory of his grandfather, the warlike Timūr (known also as Tamerlane), who had died some twenty years or so earlier. The great stone monolith was acquired as the result of a defeat inflicted on some tribes in the region north of Khotan, and it has been said that the booty had earlier come to the notice of the Chinese, who had offered a large price for it.

This last fact alone, if true and known to them, would doubtless have induced the victors to bring back the stone. However, they were already aware of its value, not only as assessed in terms of money but as the repository of numerous virtues. To the subjects of the Timurid prince it had the power "to produce rain, protect against earthquake and lightning, and to reveal, by the splitting of the vessel, any poison contained in food placed in it."[1]

Without doubt many of the merchants knew of jade from their journeyings to trade with their neighbours and others. It was the custom at the time, and later, for the more important of these missions to take the form of official embassies, and there are records of no fewer than eight of them sent from Persia and Transoxiana to China, and seven in the reverse direction between 1387 and 1432. This involved method of transacting business was described by Father Matteo Ricci, the Italian Jesuit missionary, who spent many years of his life in China.

In his memoirs written between 1608 and his death in 1610, he noted that by long-standing treaties it had been agreed with the Chinese that every five years a number of countries might send a total of seventy-two persons, conveniently designated "ambassadors," who were required to bring tribute to the emperor. The latter defrayed their expenses in both directions, and also paid the cost of the tribute as he felt it was "incompatible with his dignity to accept anything from foreigners for nothing."[2] The whole expensive undertaking was designed to impress the emperor with the fact that the world (or, at any rate, a part of it) came from time to time to pay him homage.

While the sovereign or ruler of each country selected whoever was to lead a party, the leader was allowed to choose his seventy-one companions, men who were keen to pay him for the privilege of being included. They normally returned laden with goods and with a handsome cash profit, so there was usually no lack of competition to join the embassies. Although the numbers comprising them were ostensibly limited, a well-placed bribe at the border would usually ensure entry into China of some additional persons.

Another missionary, the Portuguese Father Alvarez Semedo, gave details of what the embassies were required to proffer as tribute. He wrote: "The Merchandise which they bring, are Salt-Armoniak, fine Azure, fine linnen, carpets, called Raisins, knives, and other small things. The best and greatest Commoditie is a certain stone, called Yaca, which they bring from the Kingdom of Yauken . . .

PRINCIPAL MONGOL RULERS

Genghis Khan	1162–1227
Kublai Khan	1216–1294
Timūr (Tamerlane)	1336–1405

PRINCIPAL MUGHAL RULERS

Babar, or Baber	1526–1530
Humayun	1530–1556
Akbar	1556–1605
Jahangir	1605–1627
Jahan	1627–1658
Aurangzeb	1659–1707

The Embassadours being arrived, they offer their present, which consisteth of a thousand Arrabas of this precious stone which maketh 1333 Italian pounds, whereof 300 pounds are of the finest sort, 340 horses, which are to be left upon the frontier, 300 small pointed diamonds, twelve cattes of fine Azure, which is about 100 Italian pounds, 600 knives, & as many files."[3]

The final item worried Semedo, who could not imagine why they should be demanded or to what use files would be put. In answer, he was told that they had been included in the list long ago and no one dared to change it.

In 1419 Shah Rukh, fourth son of Timūr, sent an important embassy from

Herat, whence he had removed the capital from Samarkand, to the emperor Yung-lo. It remained in China for a year and then journeyed back by way of Khotan, so it is not at all improbable that it brought with it some stone from there. However, as in the case of the other embassies, it can be stated for certain that they took jade with them, but at present it can only be surmised whether the merchants returned with any of it.

The possibility that they may have done so is raised by the preservation in the British Museum, London, of a jade cup that can be dated positively to about the first half of the fifteenth century. It is inscribed *Ulugh Beg Gūrgān,* and was once owned by Ulugh Beg who, in 1647, succeeded his father, Shah Rukh, as Prince of Samarkand. Like his grandfather and one of his uncles, he used the title *gūrgān,* meaning son-in-law, because all three married princesses of the house of Genghis Khan. The title was adopted by Ulugh Beg in 1417, so the cup would have been his property between that date and his death in 1449, when he was murdered by his own son.

The cup is oval in shape and its handle takes the form of a tigerlike animal resembling the Chinese mythical *ch'ih,* which is found serving the same purpose on vessels of porcelain and metal made in China and elsewhere. A late twelfth or early thirteenth century Persian pottery vase in the British Museum shows that the form was not unknown in that country. The piece is of the enamelled (*minai*) type and each of the two handles is in the form of a beast. Lacking detail in the modelling, they might well be intended to represent tigers. They are seen walking up either side of the vase with their heads just about level with the rim, and one of them, if not biting the latter, is certainly sniffing at it.[4]

Two other cups, each of them light green in colour, possibly of somewhat later date than the preceding example, were presented in 1611 to the mosque at Ardebil, in northwest Persia, by Shah Abbas.[5] One of them is circular in shape with two handles, each of which is C-shaped and entwined with a grotesque animal, the rim and base being encircled by bands of incised, squared spirals. The other cup is oval, rests on four short feet, and has a carved flange protruding along the rim on each side. The handle is in the form of a tiger or dragon resting its paws and chin on the rim, while its body follows the line of the side of the cup and its tail is underneath the base. Like the other examples it is incised with squared spirals, and additionally has a band of scroll ornament. Both pieces are engraved with the word *behbūd,* which it has been suggested refers to Abū Tālib Behbūd, a name borne by two courtiers. One of them was living in about 1470 and the other a century and a half later, facts which do not assist in dating the cups. It has also been pointed out that the word *behbūd* does not necessarily represent the name of a person, but can also be an expression of approval.

These surviving pieces share a common inspiration for the design of their handles, but little more than that. The two *behbūd* cups can only be dated as some time prior to 1611, and appear to be much more akin to Chinese design and quality of workmanship than the Ulugh Beg example. In the case of the latter it has been suggested that the poor rendering of the features on the face of the *ch'ih* makes it likely that the piece was not made in China.

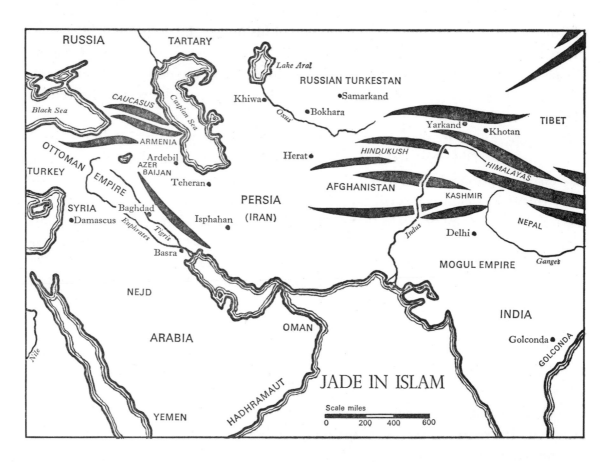

Another subject of debate on the question of origin is a group of jade articles, mostly cups and small pots, now in museums in various countries. Each is inscribed and dated, the dates falling in the first quarter of the seventeenth century, and all are made of material of a dark green colour. They are engraved with the name of Emperor Jahangir, who succeeded to the throne of his father, Akbar, at Delhi in 1605, and have little or nothing in their appearance to suggest a Chinese origin. There seems to be little doubt, however, that they were carved in India.

The Mughal dynasty was founded, following the capture of much of India, by Zahir-ud-din-Mahomet, known as Babar or Baber. A descendant of Timūr, he gained possession of Samarkand in 1497, but had it wrested from his grasp a few years later. In 1511 he recaptured it, only to be dispossessed once more. Finally, in 1526–27 Babar fought a series of battles which culminated in the establishment of his capital at Agra.

It is from the time of the great Akbar, who reigned from 1556 and completed his grandfather's conquest of the country, that the splendour of the dynasty dates. Distinguished particularly as a patron of literature, Akbar did not neglect the visual arts, and is known to have encouraged the settlement of foreign craftsmen in India. It is not known, however, that these included workers in jade.

Later, in the mid-seventeenth century, the Frenchman François Bernier, who spent twelve years in the country as physician and lived at the court of Aurangzeb, recorded what he had seen of the imperial workshops. They comprised a series of big halls resembling modern factories, to which the employees came daily from their homes. In most of these buildings a separate craft was carried on, and Bernier mentions embroidery, gold-smithing, varnishing and lacquering, and the weaving of silks and muslins, each of which had a building to itself. In another, in somewhat strange comradeship, were joiners, tailors, and shoemakers. Had jade workers been there, he might be expected to have said so, but either there were none or for some reason he did not see them. Perhaps they were established in some part of the country that Bernier did not visit during his sojourn of a dozen years.

For many centuries India has been famed for its deposits of gemstones, as well as for its native lapidaries. The inhabitants were sufficiently skilled to cut and polish diamonds, of which the Golconda mines supplied the entire ancient world. The most famous stone from Golconda is the Koh-i-noor, now one of the crown jewels of Great Britain, which legend traces back to A.D. 900 and fact to 1300. More apposite is the so-called Akbar Shah, also from Golconda, which originally weighed nearly 120 carats but was subsequently reduced to 74. Prior to being cut into the form of a drop in 1866, it was engraved with Arabic inscriptions on two of its faces. In English translation they read: "Shah Akbar, the Shah of the World, 1028" and "To the Lord of Two Worlds, Shah Jahan, 1039," the dates corresponding to A.D. 1618 and 1629.

Another diamond, larger than the preceding and at present in the Diamond

Treasury in Moscow, is the Shah, which retains engraving of about the same dates and later. While the historic Timūr Ruby, also among the British crown jewels, once belonged to Akbar's son, Jahangir, who had it inscribed with his own name and that of his father, it also bears other names and is known to have been at one time in the possession of Timūr.

Not only have Indian craftsmen a long-lasting association with precious stones, but their skill is also linked with the working of rock crystal. This is a pure form of quartz, and acquired its name from its resemblance to *crystallos:* ice. It has a hardness of 7 on the Mohs scale, which is greater than that of nephrite ($5\frac{1}{2}$ to $6\frac{1}{2}$). Rock crystal is a completely transparent and beautiful material, the forerunner and inspiration of man-made glass, and it requires a similar treatment to jade. As it is harder than the latter, it makes even greater demands on those who work it, and the same slow and painstaking processes are employed on both stones. India was one of the sources of supply of rock crystal for use by the Romans, who esteemed it highly, and it is reasonable to assume that the nation supplying the raw material also had experience in carving it.

The Timurid monarchs had a deep appreciation of jade, which is evident not only from the surviving inscribed examples but from an account given by an English traveller who visited Agra in 1609. He stated that the emperor Jahangir had "of drinking cuppes five hundred, fiftie very riche, that is to say, made of one piece of ballace ruby, and also of emerods, of eshim, of Turkish stone, and of other sorts of stones."[6] "Eshim" was a rendering of the Persian word for jade, *yashm,* but it was known also as *pād-zahr* which means literally, "counter-poison."

Living in times when turbulence was almost continual, Timūr and his followers were stern rulers, and like all despots had an ever-present fear of being given drugged food and drink—a favourite method in the Middle East of removing undesirables. The supposed property of jade as an antidote endeared it to those in power no less than its rarity and beauty. Thus, following settlement in India, their demand for cups and other articles made of the stone is readily understandable.

On present evidence it is uncertain whether they imported Persian craftsmen for the purpose, or whether the Indian lapidaries were able to adjust their skill in working rock crystal and other stones. Certainly, articles in a distinctive style were produced. Stone of an even tint was preferred, usually light in colour, white or pale green, and unlike the Chinese, who often preferred to incorporate it in a piece, they rejected the outer brown "skin." The jade was fashioned into objects with noticeably thin walls; and carving, when there is any, is in low relief so that the subtle markings which give the stone its character are fully visible. Comparison with pieces made of rock crystal shows that the jades have similar features, so that it is perfectly possible that both emanated from the same workshops, if not the selfsame hands.

The most beautiful of surviving Mughal jades—a piece exhibiting the highest degree of craftsmanship—is the wine-cup (Plate 136), which once belonged to Shah Jahan and is now in the Victoria and Albert Museum, London. It was once accepted unhesitatingly as eighteenth-century Chinese work, "on the uncritical assumption," in the words of John Irwin, "that only the Chinese were capable of such a masterpiece." Then it was found to be inscribed neatly and unobtrusively in Persian with Shah Jahan's title and the equivalent of the date A.D. 1657 (Plate 137).

It has been shown that the cup embodies in its design elements from several countries:[7] the bowl from a Chinese gourd, the tapered shape from Persian metalwork, and the handle from Europe—all of them blended in the Indian manner of the time. The base of the cup is a six-petalled lotus flower, a common Eastern motif, while the lower part of the bowl is carved with eight acanthus leaves. These had once been a familiar feature of the Indian decorative repertoire, but their use had died out a thousand years or so before. Their revival in the late seventeenth century may be attributed to the influence of the many foreigners, including Europeans, working for the court.

Other countries using jade were content to leave the stone unadorned, relying on the colour and marking of the stone with little or much carving, according to taste, to complete it. The Indians, however, frequently embellished their work by inlaying it with precious and semiprecious stones set in gold. The effect is often rich and dazzling, but to eyes attuned to the dignified calm of jade itself it may often seem that the Mughal craftsmen were merely gilding the lily. Occasionally such work took the form of no more than a ruby or two neatly inserted in a handle, but more frequently the whole surface of an object was covered in a network of gold, glittering with points of diamond and colour. The surface of the stone having been cut into as required, the incisions and cavities were filled with pure gold and the stones held in place by the latter.

Inlaying stone in stone was not unknown in India at the time of Shah Jahan, and is employed with considerable effect in the Taj Mahal at Agra. The building was erected between 1630 and 1652 at the behest of Shah Jahan to serve as a mausoleum for his wife Muntaz-i-Mahal ("Jewel of the Palace"), who had died in

1629. Her sarcophagus stands next to that of her husband, who died in 1666, and both are encircled by a pierced and inlaid marble screen. Not only is the inlay a reflection of the more glittering work found on jade, but its pattern of flowers and leafy scrolls is also paralleled in jade designs.

Similarly ornamented is the Diwan-i-Am, the public audience chamber in the buildings of the Red Fort at Delhi. The room encloses a tomblike, canopied structure of marble, the upper portion of which is inlaid while the deep base is carved in low relief. The carving is designed as shaped panels of flowers and leaves flanked by fluted balustroid columns, and the remaining spaces are also filled with floral designs.

A keen interest in flowers and floral patterns was in evidence in Europe during the period when the Taj Mahal was under construction. The origins of the interest can be traced back to the late sixteenth century, when the gardens and hothouses in Paris, later to become the Jardin des Plantes, were first established. Under King Henry IV, they became famous for the rarities they contained, which were brought to the city from all over the world. The peak of this admiration in the West was the "tulipomania" that overtook Holland, and which, after a few years of feverish speculation, collapsed in 1637. The movement is exemplified in the large number of flower paintings surviving from the period, by printed herbals and botanical books, and by engraved designs for jewellery. The latter, of which many originated in France, showed that there was a liking for the curving lines of stylised naturalism enclosed within leaf-shaped outlines.[8] The mode is to be seen not only in such objects as the diamond-set brooches worn by ladies at the courts of France and other countries, but many thousands of miles away in the decorations on the walls of the Taj Mahal. Even the carpets on its floors were woven with sprays of lilies, carnations, tulips, and roses blossoming on brightly coloured grounds. Flower and leaf shapes also outline many of the precious-stone and gold inlays in the jade of the period, giving the articles a flamboyance in which the wealth of the Mughal Empire and its rulers is paradoxically linked with the simple forms of nature.

The empire began to decline during the lengthy reign of Aurangzeb, third son of Shah Jahan, who occupied the throne during the years 1659–1707. Just over thirty years after his death, the Persian Nadir Shah captured and sacked Delhi, an event which heralded the demise of a regime that had been looked upon for two centuries as the source of untold riches.

While some of the surviving examples of inlaid Mughal jade date from the seventeenth century, most are later. The workshops must have carried on largely unhampered by the upheavals that disturbed the country from the early 1700s onward, and the same techniques were practised well into the reign of Queen Victoria when India was under British rule. Accidentally or deliberately, in some instances the valuable stones were removed and have been replaced at a later date by indifferent or poor ones; a fact that is usually revealed by a careful inspection.

Some specimens of the thin-walled carved jade from India reached China, and at least three pieces were seen by the Emperor Ch'ien-lung and duly inscribed with poems from his facile brush. One verse, included in the collection of imperial poems, is entitled "Lines on a Jar from Hindustan," so there was no doubt at the time about where the piece was made.

There are a number of existing pieces of jade which are carved in the Indian manner, but are very much in the Chinese style. Various arguments have been put forward to account for them, but none has yet been proved conclusive. It is said that while the original Indian-style pieces were made in India and some were sent to Peking, they so captivated the inhabitants there that the craftsmen in the imperial workshops were given the task of imitating them. As the more sophisticated Chinese are known to have been fond of foreign innovations of many kinds —watches and clocks being high on the list, and the subject of close imitation— it is not at all improbable that this unusual type of carved work would have intrigued them and inspired a similar copying.

It has also been suggested that all such carving was executed in India where a number of Chinese workers were responsible for it. The theory is that they went to India during the seventeenth century, when the scarcity of identified examples of Chinese jade suggests that the art was far from flourishing in that country. The workers might therefore have been willing to seek employment at their craft in another land, and the fact that Indian jade does not seem to predate the seventeenth century has been adduced in support of the theory.

Perhaps positive evidence will be found one day to settle beyond any doubt what really occurred, but in the meantime there seems no reason not to accept that the Indians carved jade in their own style, and the Chinese duly copied it in the *Hsi fan tso* (the Indian school) in Peking. Whether the Indian craftsmen used their native talents as lapidaries for their work, or were dependent, to a great or less degree, on carvers from Persia also awaits clarification.

The inlaying of jade with precious stones was not confined to India. The scimitar illustrated in Plate 140 has a handle of Indian jade encrusted to match the steel blade, the work having been executed in Turkey. Craftsmen in that country were readily available, as such lavish embellishment was much to the taste of the court. Their admiration for imported Chinese porcelain led the Turks to embellish it in a similar manner, cutting through the glaze for the insertion of gold, which was then inset with stones.[9] As the hardness of the ware varied between six and seven on the Mohs scale, similar incisions in jade would have presented no difficulty. Moreover, jade would have been incomparably easier to handle, for the likelihood of a porcelain article fracturing in the course of the work was ever-present and much more probable than the breakage of a piece of jade.

CHAPTER FIVE

JAPANESE AND KOREAN JADE

SMALL jade objects have been found in Japanese graves of the second and third centuries A.D. and earlier, and are variously of nephrite and jadeite with, surprisingly enough, jadeite predominating. The majority of the finds take the form of curved beads, rather like thickened commas and known as *magatama,* which measure about four centimetres overall in length. Others are tubular beads (*kudatama*), and yet others, the most scarce of all, are flat pendants.

The *magatama,* which were made also of many different kinds of stone and of coloured glass, were amulets associated with the Shintō goddess of the sun, Amaterasu, whose grandson was the legendary first ruler of Japan. They were worn on the body, either round the neck, suspended from the ears, or on armlets. They have also been found affixed to head ornaments. In the sphere of legend, the gods were said to have owned swords covered with them. The custom of placing in a grave the *magatama* worn by the deceased in his lifetime was discontinued following the introduction of Buddhism into the country, at which time lavish funerals were forbidden.

The sources of the jade used for the various objects would seem to have been China in the case of the nephrite, and Japan itself for the jadeite. In the present century jadeite has been discovered in the Kotaki district of Niigata Prefecture, and a report published in 1953 stated that although "the veins of jadeite were thin and the quality of the material not high, they would have been sufficient for a bead-making industry."[1] Prior to this discovery it had been supposed that the articles in question were made of a stone merely resembling jadeite in appearance, because jadeite was unknown to the Chinese before the late eighteenth century and could not have reached Japan from Burma prior to that date. It would not have been possible for the Japanese to have had access to Burmese jadeite without the Chinese knowing about it.

The nephrite objects, which form a minor proportion of extant specimens, must have been carved from pieces of the stone exported from China, whence it had arrived from Khotan. It is not unlikely, however, that *magatama* and other items were exported ready-made by way of Shanghai or some southern Chinese port.

Jade carving was no less tedious and time-consuming in Japan than elsewhere. Sand, water, and infinite patience were essential, but doubtless because supplies of the stone, whether native or imported, were so short, the output was re-

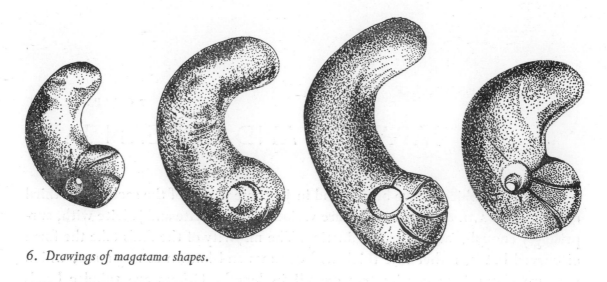

6. *Drawings of magatama shapes.*

stricted in both quantity and design. The pendants and other ornaments cannot compare artistically with Chinese products of the same period, but the Japanese would appear to have reserved the material solely for making simple amulets and did not attempt anything of significant design.

A few jade netsuke, the toggles which hold possessions securely to the girdle of the kimono, have been recorded. Netsuke were carved in wood, ivory, or bone, and were the work of highly respected artists who flourished in numerous centres of production. The jade examples may have been made to order and imported from China or, less probably, the raw stone from there may have been carved in Japan. A site of manufacture in Japan is less likely because of the absence of evidence of the existence of skilled craftsmen to do such work in Tokyo, Kyoto, or anywhere else in the islands.

Magatama have been found abundantly in graves in Korea, a country with which Japan had close cultural ties until the first millenium A.D., when Chinese influence became paramount. The beads were more common in Korea, and they continued to be worn there long after the custom had ceased to be general in Japan. Of surviving jade specimens a number were found embellishing an important gold crown, excavated at Kyongju, which was once the capital of the Korean kingdom of Silla. The crown is attributed to the sixth or seventh century A.D., and was one of the most admired objects in the exhibition of National Art Treasures of Korea, held at the Victoria and Albert Museum, London, in 1961.[2]

In the same display, and likewise from the tomb at Kyongju, was a girdle hung with ornaments of gold, glass, and jade. Two of these were *magatama,* while others were of different shapes including some in the form of fishes. Both the crown and the girdle are in the National Museum of Korea, but while they were in England Professor Hansford seized the opportunity to gain permission to have a *magatama* from the crown tested. It proved to be jadeite, and it is probable that at some time in the future a Korean source for this stone, albeit not comparable in output with Burma, will come to light.

OTHER EASTERN JADE

131–32. *Two views of the jade tomb of Timūr who died in 1405 (centre), in the Gur Emir, Samarkand. The jade is dark green and inscribed in Arabic with the words: "When I rise from the dead, the world will tremble." Photos: Plate 131, Inge Morath, Magnum; Plate 132, John Massey Stewart.*

133. *Jug incised with an overall pattern of leafy scrolls, the handle in the form of a stylised animal. Dark green, parcel-gilt. Sixteenth century. Freer Gallery of Art, Washington, D.C.*

136. Drinking cup, formerly in the possession of Shah Jahan. The body of the cup is ▷
gourd shaped with the base in the form of a lotus blossom; the handle is shaped as the
head of an ibex. The cup is dated by an inscription in Arabic equivalent to 1657. White.
Length, 19 cm. Victoria & Albert Museum, London.

134. Powder flask carved with an animal head at either end, mounted in gold, and inset with
rubies. Pale greenish grey with markings ranging from grey to brown. Eighteenth century. Length,
14 cm. Victoria & Albert Museum, London.

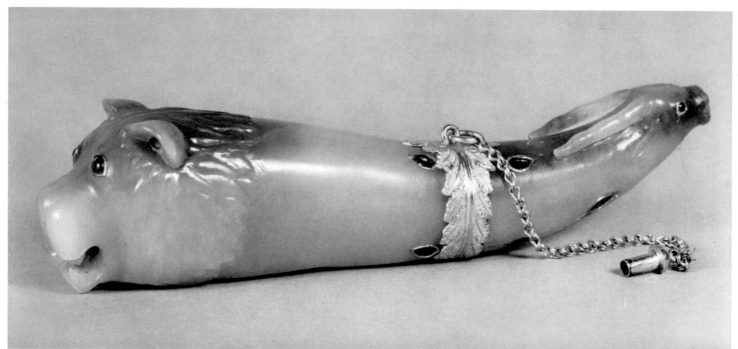

135. Drinking bowl carved with flowers. The two handles are in the form of birds' heads with eyes of inset
rubies. Light green. Late seventeenth century. Length, 21.6 cm. Victoria & Albert Museum, London.

137. Detail of the inscription on Shah Jahan's cup. It records his title, "The Second Lord ▷
of the Conjunction," and the year 1067 of the Moslem era, corresponding to A.D. 1657

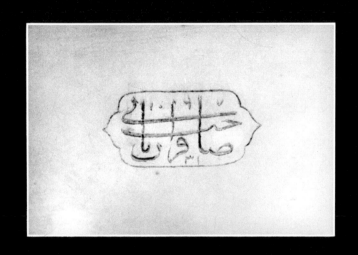

158

138–39. *Front and back of a mirror case, carved and pierced, inlaid with gold and inset with rubies. Seventeenth century. 16.2 × 10.1 cm. Seattle Art Museum, Eugene Fuller Memorial Collection. (See page 153 for detail.)*

159

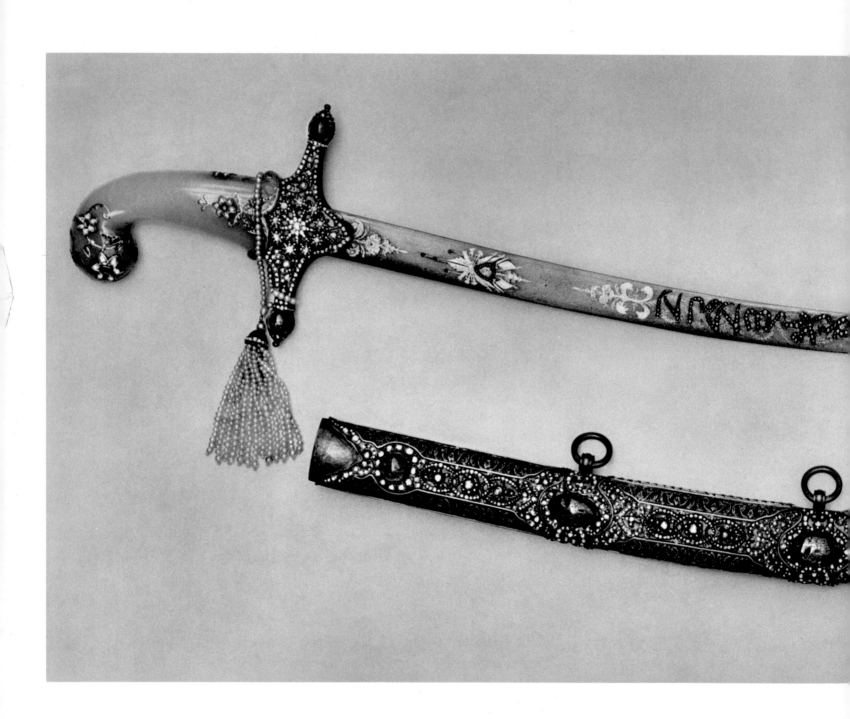

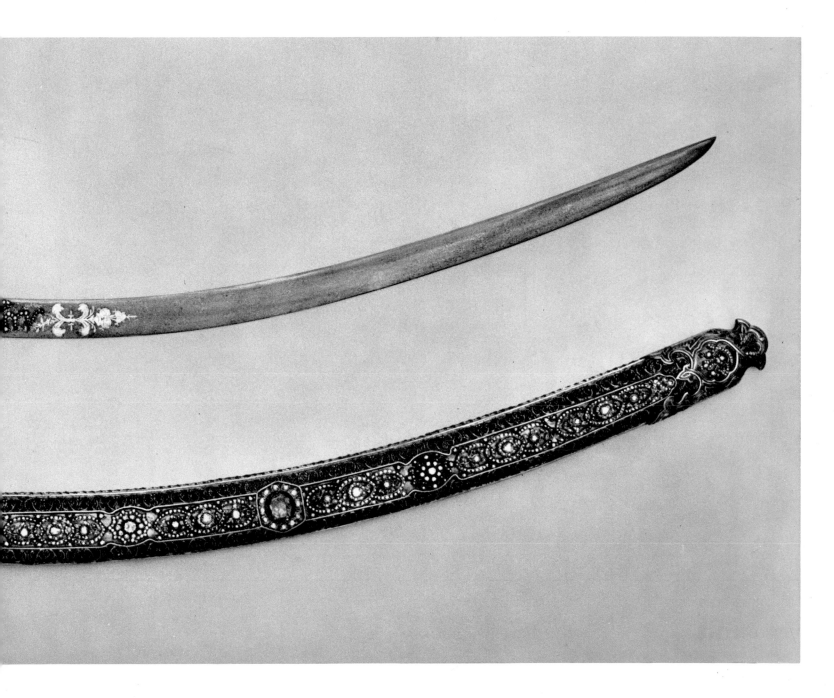

140. *Scimitar and scabbard. The hilt is of pale green jade inset with diamonds. Overall length, 100 cm. This is the state sword of Murad V, sultan of Turkey from May until September, 1876. The blade is dated 1099 A.H. (1688 A.D.), and both it and the scabbard bear gold-damascened pious inscriptions. The scabbard is signed: "Made by Musa." The blade was made in Persia but its ornamentation, as well as that on the scabbard and on the eighteenth-century (?) Indian jade hilt, was added in the nineteenth century. Metropolitan Museum of Art, New York. Gift of Giulia P. Morosini, 1923.*

141. *Dagger and scabbard mounted in white jade with diamonds, rubies, and emeralds inset in gold. Eighteenth century. Length, about 43 cm. Victoria & Albert Museum, London.*

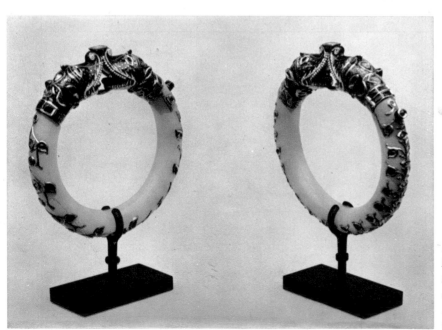

142. *Dagger hilt of dark sage-green jade inlaid with a floral pattern in silver. Eighteenth century. Length, 10.5 cm. Metropolitan Museum of Art, New York. Gift of Heber R. Bishop, 1902.*

143. *Pair of armlets of white jade inlaid with gold and inset with diamonds, rubies, and emeralds. The armlets are mounted with gold terminals enamelled red, blue, and green, and formed as conjoined dragons' heads. Seventeenth century. Diameter, 7.9 cm. Metropolitan Museum of Art, New York. Gift of Heber R. Bishop, 1902.*

145. Six-lobed bowl. Each lobe is carved on the inside with a floral design, and the base is an open flower. Opalescent yellowish grey. Seventeenth century. Diameter, 17 cm. Metropolitan Museum of Art, New York. Gift of Heber R. Bishop, 1902.

146. Bowl carved in low relief with floral sprays and with scrolling leaves and flower heads from which hang loose rings. Pale grey. Eighteenth century. Width, 20.3 cm. Spink & Son, London.

147. *Vase and cover with loose rings hanging from leafy scrolls. Inset with rubies mounted in gold. Green. Eighteenth century. Height 17.1 cm. Christie's, London.*

148. *A pendant. Jadeite. About 2000–1000* B.C. *Length, 7.3 cm.; thickness, 1 cm. Found in Tochigi Prefecture, not far from Tokyo. Tokyo National Museum.*

149. *A pendant. Jadeite. About 2000–1000* B.C. *Length, 11.3 cm., thickness, 1 cm. Found in Gumma Prefecture, not far from Tokyo. Tokyo National Museum. (See Plate 2 for detail.)*

150. Amulet (heitiki), with a perforated lug for suspension. Green. Height, 9.5 cm. Formerly in the Mackay Collection, from Pahia, near Invercargill. Otago Museum, Dunedin, New Zealand.

151. *A New Zealander, tattooed, and wearing a jade ear ornament* (kurukuru) *and an amulet* (heitiki). *Engraving illustrating* An Epitome of Lieut. Cook's Voyage round the World, *published in* The Gentleman's Magazine, *Vol. 44 (January, 1774).*

152. *Amulet* (heitiki). *Pale leaf green, the eyes inlaid with paua shell. Length, 17.4 cm. Metropolitan Museum of Art, New York. Gift of Heber R. Bishop, 1902.*

153. Amulet (heitiki). *Pale green ranging to near white. Length, 13.5 cm. From the Thomson collection. Otago Museum, Dunedin, New Zealand.*

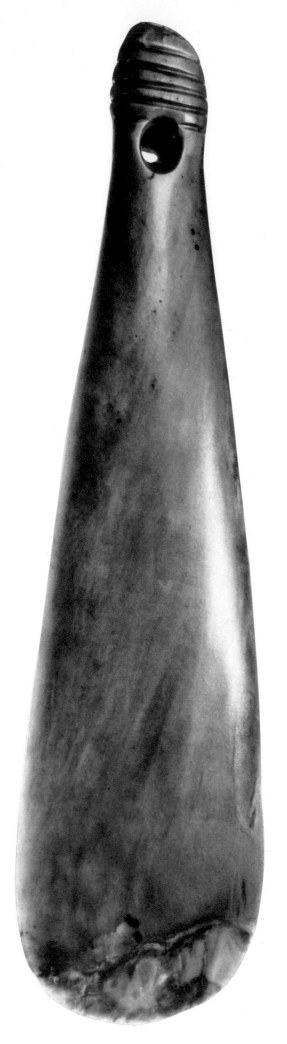

154. Club (mere pounamu). *Formerly an heirloom of the Parata family of Otago, known by the name Tira and traced back through ten generations by its last owner. Length, 42 cm.; greatest width, 12 cm. Otago Museum, Dunedin, New Zealand.*

155. Adze (toki pounamu), *carved with lugs to retain the lashing with which it was attached to a wooden handle. Length, 32.5 cm. Found at Portobello, near Dunedin, and adjudged as perhaps the finest known example. Otago Museum, Dunedin, New Zealand.*

156. *Ritual adze (toki poutangata). Wood handle carved and inlaid. Blade length, 28.5 cm. Otago Museum, Dunedin, New Zealand.*

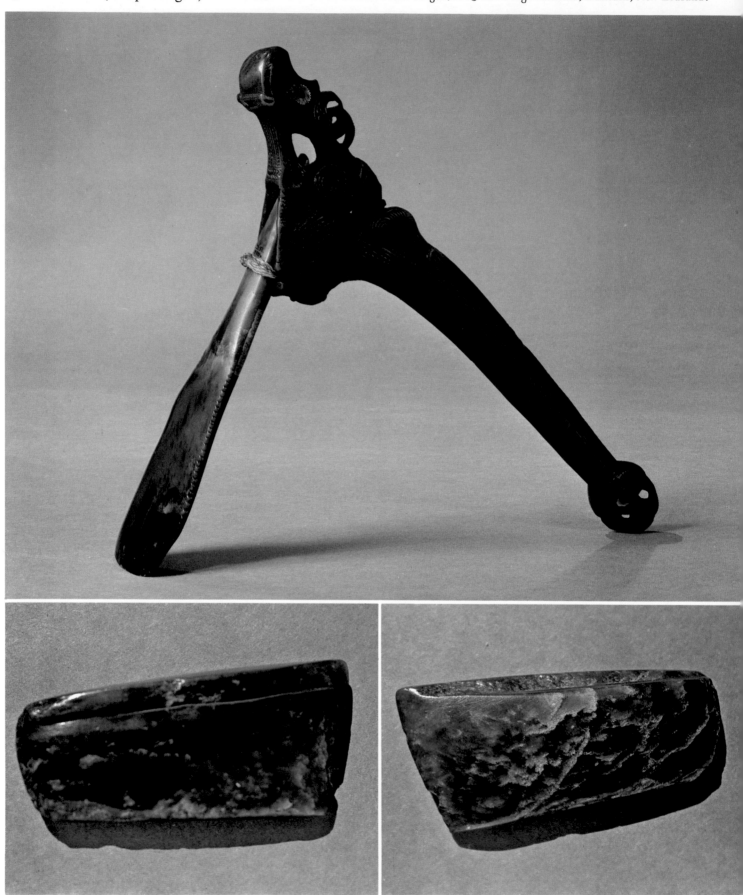

157–58. *Cutting tool. Length, 8.9 cm. Private collection.*

160. *Amulet (pekapeka) in the form of interlaced scrolls with what appear to be masks at either end, derived from the bird-man Manaia. Found buried with a skeleton in sandhills near Kaitaia at the north of North Island. Width, 6 cm. Otago Museum, Dunedin, New Zealand.*

161. *Pendant* (heimatau) *in the form of a fish-hook.* 4 × 3.5 cm. Otago Museum, Dunedin, New Zealand.

162. *Adze (toki pounamu). Dark and light shades of green. Length of blade,*
10.2 cm. Metropolitan Museum of Art, New York. Gift of Heber R. Bishop, 1902.

CHAPTER SIX

NEW ZEALAND JADE

IN THE year 1642, a Dutchman named Abel Jansen Tasman chanced on the islands now called New Zealand as he explored this uncharted area of the ocean in the Dutch East India Company's ship *Heemskerk*. Setting out from the newly-named Van Dieman's Land (later named Tasmania after him), he sailed on December 5 on an easterly course for the Solomon Islands. Seven days later, he wrote in his account of the voyage, "I discovered a high mountainous country." And he called this place Staten Landt—Land of the States, or Holland. The name was later altered to New Zealand.

On December 18, Tasman dropped anchor in what is now Cook Strait, the channel between North and South Islands, but he mistook it for "a fine bay." Here, he noted: "We found . . . abundance of the inhabitants: they had very hoarse voices, and were very large-made people. They durst not approach the ship nearer than a stone's throw; and we often observed them playing on a kind of trumpet, to which we answered with the instruments that were on board our vessel. These people were of a colour between brown and yellow, their hair long, and almost as thick as that of the Japanese, combed up and fixed on the top of their heads, with a quill, or some such thing . . . These people cover the middle of their bodies, some with a kind of mat, others with a sort of woollen cloth; but, as for their upper and lower parts, they leave them altogether naked."[1]

On the following day, Tasman was apparently on board the accompanying vessel, the *Zeehaen*, when he noticed that some of the natives had gone out to the *Heemskerk*. Anxious in case they should surprise and attack the crew, he despatched seven men to row across and warn them, but the men were set on by the New Zealanders and three of the Dutch were killed. Tasman commented, "Our ship's company would, undoubtedly, have taken a severe revenge, if the rough weather had not hindered them."

Sailing along the coast, the Dutch came to the northern tip of the North Island, where they thought of making a landing. But recent experience had made them cautious, and it was obvious that the inhabitants had noticed their arrival offshore. Tasman wrote: "As we approached it, we perceived on the mountain thirty or five-and-thirty persons, who, as far as we could discern at such a distance, were men of very large size, and had each of them a large club in his hand; they called out to us in a rough strong voice, but we could not understand any thing of what they said." Exercising discretion, the *Heemskerk* and the *Zeehaen* sailed away without anyone setting foot on the land, and without realising that the country comprised two separate large islands.

A hundred and twenty-seven years were to elapse before another European reached New Zealand, and then the explorer was an Englishman, Captain James Cook. He arrived on October 7, 1769 in the barque *Endeavour,* having sailed from the Thames in August of the preceding year, accompanied by a carefully selected party which included Joseph Banks, the naturalist, and Dr. Carl Solander, the Swedish-born botanist. On this occasion, a landing was made, but the natives proved no friendlier than they had done earlier. No doubt to prove the point, Banks was presented by one of them with a human arm-bone, "and to show us

---

CHRONOLOGICAL TABLE OF EVENTS

1642	Abel Jansen Tasman of Holland discovers "a high mountainous country," which he names Staten Landt (Land of the States)
1769	Captain James Cook circumnavigates the two islands, charts the waters, and lands at various points
1814	Arrival of missionaries from England
1840	The country comes under the sovereignty of Queen Victoria
1852	Self-government granted

---

that they eat the flesh, they bit and gnaw'd the bone and draw'd it through their mouths and this in such a manner as plainly shewed that the flesh to them was a dainty bit."

Later in the same month Cook went with Banks and Solander to try and establish friendly relations, but it was in vain. The visitors were forced to use their firearms in self-defence. Yet, when they landed elsewhere in the country during their six months' exploration of the coast, they were better treated. Banks recorded, doubtless with relief: "When we went into their homes, men, women and children received us; no-one showed the least sign of fear. The women were as coquettish as any European could be and the young ones as skittish as un-broken fillies."[2]

The Maori inhabitants of New Zealand were descended from Polynesians who came in their canoes from distant islands, supplanting the people already living there. By at least the fourteenth century A.D., the newcomers had colonised the North Island, and by the time of Tasman's arrival in 1642, they had spread farther afield to the South Island. It was the descendants of the South Island people that Cook's party found so amiable.

The source of New Zealand jade lay in the South Island, on the west coast to the north of Westland, which is bordered on one side by the Pacific and on the other by the extensive and precipitous Southern Alps. The stone was found in the valleys through which flowed the rivers Taramakau and Arahura, and on the beaches where they entered the sea. Not until the present century were actual veins of the material located, and it is accepted that the Maoris relied on the chance finding of boulders and pebbles washed down from the mountains. They were apparently ignorant of whence these came, and there is no record of wheth-er they ever sought their true source high in the Griffin Range.

The stone is nephrite, known to the natives by the name of *pounamu,* and to later settlers from Europe as "greenstone." It ranges in colour from greyish white to black, with a preponderance of a rich darkish green which often shows cloudlike markings. It is hard and heavy, and shares the characteristics of the variety from East Turkestan. The Maoris distinguished half a dozen varieties of the stone, of which a pale translucent green, *kahurangi,* is the rarest. They named a grey kind *inanga,* and the dark green noted above was called *kawakawa;* yet another with distinctive flecks was called *tangiwai,* (weeping water). It acquired its name because it was supposed to represent the body of the missing wife of a famous native explorer whose tears, when he found her corpse, gave the stone its characteristic teardrop markings.

Jade was esteemed by the Maoris no less than it was by the Chinese, and with both races it is probable that the rarity of the stone, as much as its beauty and durability, was an important factor in its appeal. While at first it was no doubt worked close to where it was found, in time the material was traded to craftsmen in the North Island. There is no certain way of differentiating between fin-ished examples from one place or another, although it is considered that in the north, the first area to be colonised, the artistic standards of the inhabitants were higher and the better designed and better finished work was done there.

No metal was known to the New Zealanders until Cook called there in 1769, and until that date, and indeed for a long time afterward, none was used. The working of jade and other materials was carried out entirely by means of tools made of wood, bone, stone, or shell. Sand was the cutting medium, and with the

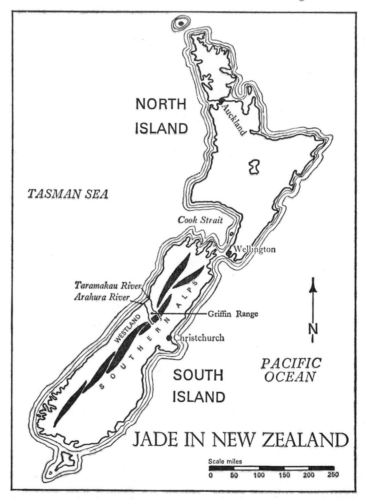

addition of water it was laboriously employed. A cut was made on either side of a slab of greenstone, and after sufficiently deep grooves had been made a sharp tap finished the task and the stone was split.

A report written by an Englishman in 1846 records the arduous business of making holes: "For this, pieces of sharp flint are obtained from the Pahutani cliff, forty miles to the north, and are set in the end of a split stick, being lashed in very neatly. The stick is about 15 in. to 18 in. [38 to 45 cm.] long, and is to become the spindle of a large teetotum drill. For the circular plate of this instrument, the hardened invertebral cartilage of a whale is taken. A hole is made through, and the stick firmly and accurately fixed in it. Two strings are then attached to the upper end of the stick, and by pulling them a rapid motion is given to the drill. When an indentation is once made in the *pounamu,* the work is easy. As each flint becomes blunted it is replaced by another in the stick until the work is done."[3]

Another account, published in 1852, stated that two stones were lashed to the upright spindle. They acted as a flywheel to assist momentum, while at the same time their weight helped to keep the drill in the desired position. The apparatus was rotated by means of a length of cord wound a few times round the spindle, which gave the whole a reciprocal action as each end was pulled in turn. Hole making was a very slow process indeed. As with cutting, the work was done from both sides to meet, more or less, in the middle, and the apertures on the surface are invariably tapered and untidy.

No doubt individual craftsmen had their own methods and there was a continual, if slow, seeking after improvements. Anything to lessen labour and the time expended must have been welcomed, but on the whole, allowing for the small variety of suitable tools at hand, little progress could be made. The craftsmen observed and reported on by mid-nineteenth century visitors were probably employing techniques little, if at all, different from those of the Maoris who first found the stone.

The number of different articles made from jade by the Maoris is not very large, and includes some that were used daily as tools and weapons, and a few of which the function was purely ceremonial or decorative. In the daily-use category are blades for chisels, axes, and adzes—implements highly important for existence in a densely forested land. The adze (*toki*) differs from the more familiar axe in having its blade set at right angles to the handle, and was employed for the same purpose as a modern carpenter's plane. In place of a blade held in a box and slid across the surface of a piece of timber, the adze was used with a swinging motion. The blade, sharpened as much as possible at one end, usually had a hole drilled through the other and was fastened to a handle about thirty-eight to forty-five centimetres long. It was held firmly in place by a cord, which was threaded through the hole and bound tightly round both jade and wooden components. The weight of the stone assisted the user as he swung the instrument back and forth, chipping away at a log or plank. The blades of these adzes vary in length, and a large-sized specimen may measure up to forty-five centimetres, with a width of ten to thirteen centimetres. The weight may be as much as two kilograms.

Although it was basically a tool, the *toki* had another function, that of a baton or symbol of rank. It would be carried by a chief to signify his importance, and he would brandish it during speech making to emphasize his words. A ceremonial adze is shown in Plate 156. The jade blade has a serrated edge and is bound to a wooden handle, which is carved with a formal human figure inset with shell to mark the eyes. The ball-like handgrip is further inset with shell, and is drilled with two holes for a wrist loop. No doubt this piece was once a treasured possession and was passed down from generation to generation in a chief's family. It was brought to England in the mid-nineteenth century, but unfortunately nothing is known of its earlier history. In 1950 it was acquired by the Otago Museum and returned to New Zealand.

Blades a few inches in length were required for more intricate work than could be performed with the adze. Chisels (*whao*) of this type might be hand held or lashed securely to a short handle of wood, but in either instance they were probably too blunt to be effectively used without being tapped with a hammer. The double-edged axe was also a Maori tool, but few examples are known. Besides the more usual adzes and chisels, there is a greenstone cutter, tapered in form, with the wide end sharpened and sloping, while the narrow end shows clear signs of having originally been used with a hammer of some kind. The surface on one side is grooved near the top or longer side, whereas the other has a roughly finished channel (Plates 157 and 158).

The warlike Maoris used greenstone in making one of their favourite weapons, the *mere* or *patoo-patoo*—a shorthandled club with a flat, thin-edged, oval-ended blade. For defence or offence the small size of these clubs enabled them to be concealed under a cloak and then brought forth swiftly for hand-to-hand encounters. Jade examples were confined mainly to tribal chiefs, lower-ranking men having to be content with whalebone or wood; but whatever the material, they were efficient in use. The *mere pounamu* was regarded also as a symbol of authority, like the adze, and in that role it paralleled an ancient Chinese use of jade.

The major part of the *mere,* which measures overall about thirty-eight centimetres in length and about nine centimetres in width, is plain and polished. The butt of the handle usually takes the form of a knob with a series of ridges and furrows running round it, and is pierced with a hole. Through this was threaded a wriststrap made of flax cord or hide—the latter made of dog or human skin to suit the preference of the owner.

There is a graphic description of the use of the *mere* as seen during one of Captain Cook's landings. In the record of his voyage printed serially in issues of the *Gentleman's Magazine* in 1773 and 1774, it is noted that a party of belligerent natives was armed with "long pikes . . . and short truncheons of green talk [*sic*] polished, weighing from 4 to 5 pounds." On a later occasion there was an arresting demonstration of the effectiveness of the weapon, which seems to have impressed the audience: "Mr Banks's party were met by an old warrior, who diverted them with a sham attack after his country manner; a post was his adversary, and a lance and pata-patoo were his weapons; the lance was about twelve feet long [3.7 metres], and the pata-patoo about fifteen inches [thirty-eight centimetres] in shape like a battledore, with the broad end sharpened all round to an edge, and the handle finely polished. He first attacked the post with his lance, and having pierced it, fell upon it with his pata-patoo, cleaving it at every stroke, to shew the manners of cleaving the head of an enemy. The pata-patoo appears to be a more deadly weapon than even the tomahawk of the Indians of North America; and as the North-American Indian plumes himself upon the scalps of his enemy, so these warriors carry off in triumph the jawbones."[4]

The best known of all New Zealand jade objects is the ornamental pendant known as a *heitiki*: a neck ornament based on the mythological Tiki. It is in the shape of a grotesque foetuslike figure with an oversize head, the chin resting to right, left or centre, and is roughly rectangular overall. The large eyes are surrounded by circular ridges or furrows, which increase the curious appearance of the object. If encircled by furrows, the studlike eyeballs are emphasised by inlays of red sealingwax or shaped fragments of pearllike seashell (*paua*). The arms bend inwards at the elbows and the legs are folded to meet at the feet, but usually neither hands nor feet are indicated. Only in rare instances is there any detailed workmanship, but considering the lack of tools for carving this is hardly surprising.

The origins and significance of Tiki are debatable. According to Maori belief he was the first man, and was formed by Tu-matauenga, the god of war and mankind; a thought-provoking combination. He created a woman, and his image is said to have phallic significance. The resemblance to an embryo is apparently accidental, and has not been explained satisfactorily. It has been suggested that the *heitiki* was worn as a fertility amulet, but any adornment, whether of jade or some other material, has been said at one time or another to have conferred this much-sought capability.

The *heitiki* was worn at the neck, suspended from a cord of woven flax. One end of the cord was looped and the other ended in a bone toggle, which fitted through the loop to hold the pendant in place. When a chief died, his *heitiki* and his weapons were placed beside the body and buried with it, but after a period of years, during which the flesh had decomposed, the bones together with his possessions were recovered. His friends would gather to mourn his loss and re-collect his character, deeds, and sayings, while his *heitiki* lay before them where 't had been placed reverentially on the ground. As an heirloom it was prized by his descendants, and ownership of an historic example conferred great prestige.

The majority of them measure on average seven by five centimetres, but very much larger ones are known. An exceptional *heitiki* with a length of almost twenty-three centimetres was sold by Sotheby's in London in the 1960s and purchased on behalf of the New Zealand government. While it is true that the older examples are usually of small size, it cannot be said that all small ones are old. Equally, large specimens vary in their age, and each must be judged on its merits.

The Maoris did not consider size as the criterion of a good *heitiki;* the big ones would have been awkward to wear. It was Europeans who, in the course of the nineteenth century, demanded the large examples and for whom most of them were made. The visitors were responsible for the widespread use of metal tools in the country, and this made redundant most of the jade axes, chisels, and adzes. The blades of these now-useless objects were a convenient source of the stone, and many of them were then skillfully reshaped into *heitiki*. The bigger the *heitiki,* the more impressed and pleased were the buyers.

Other articles made of jade by the Maoris were ear pendants, fish-hooks, leg rings for parrots and, almost unbelievably, needles. A recorded specimen of the last is twenty-three centimetres in length and six millimetres in diameter. It is most likely that the hole for the eye was drilled before the shaping was completed, and possibly before the selected sliver was cut from the slab of stone.

Ear ornaments varied in form, rodlike examples being the most popular. These have a hole drilled at one end, while the other is a blunted point (*kurukuru*), or is curved (*tautau*). Their length ranges from seven to twenty centimetres, with the weight of the latter putting a considerable strain on the earlobes of the wearer. Other shapes of ear ornaments were circular, although more so by intent than in execution, and there are U-shaped pieces. Some rare specimens of the latter have one of the upright arms shaped at the top to resemble the head of a bird, and are a reminder that a real bird was an occasional adornment of both sexes. The head of the live victim was forced through a hole in the earlobe, and kept there long after the bird had given up trying to escape and was dead.[5]

Another variety (*pekapeka*), which is very much scarcer in old examples than in new, is carved with a stylised representation of two entwined figures of Manaia. This is a strange figure half-way between a bird and a human, and sometimes described as a birdlike man. Manaia resembles Tiki, with three fingers on each hand and three toes on each foot, and its origin and meaning are no less the subject of speculation than are those of Tiki.

The jade leg ring for a parrot, known as *kaka-poria,* comprises two rings joined together, one of greater diameter than the other, the larger of them having three or four sets of small projections round the edge. The bird's leg was held in the bigger ring and a cord was attached to the other one. It has been suggested that they were made at first for the purpose which gave them their name, but that later ones were only decorative articles resembling the *kaka-poria* in appearance and given the same name.[6]

Jade fish-hooks (*matau*), which may be considered to have been reserved for special occasions and then used only by the most favoured of fishermen, resemble normal modern ones in having a barb. A recorded example with an overall size of thirty-two by twenty-one millimetres has a groove running round the lower part of the curve, and the edges are finely serrated.

A further potential link with Chinese usage is the possibility that the musical quality of jade was appreciated by the Maoris. A fortified village (*pa*) was guarded constantly by sentries who, if an attack was imminent, would raise the alarm by striking a gong made of hardwood. At the *pa* at Maungakiekie (One Tree Hill, on the outskirts of the city of Auckland, North Island) the gong is traditionally said to have been a piece of greenstone, but while this is by no means improbable, it remains unproved. In the same way as many other legends of the country have subsequently been found to have a basis of fact, this one may some day be revealed as equally credible.

New Zealand jade understandably has a great interest for the inhabitants of the country, for it epitomises Maori history and culture. In addition, the stone and its working have been studied far and wide in conjunction with research into early Chinese nephrite. The fact that the Maoris remained untouched by outside contact until the second half of the eighteenth century, has enabled illuminating parallels to be drawn between their civilisation and that of the ancient Chinese.

NOTES

In the following notes, sources are referred to by author or short title alone or, in some cases, by author and date of publication. Full publishing information concerning these works is given in the Bibliography.

CHAPTER 1

1. Hansford (1968), p. 39 and plates C and D.
2. Hansford (1950), pp. 32–34.
3. Hansford (1950), pp. 51–53.
4. Griffith, p. 132.
5. Chhibber, p. 64.
6. Mr. Warry's report of his visit is reprinted in *Gazetteer of Upper Burma* and also in Hertz, vol. A.
7. Hansford (1950), p. 45.
8. Chhibber, pp. 79–80.
9. Burton, p. 93.
10. Barrow, see under Jade in vol. 2.
11. Yule, p. 277.

CHAPTER 2

1. One of these drawings and a detail from another are reproduced in Palmer.
2. Laufer, p. 9.
3. Hansford (1950), pp. 5–11, figs. 1–6.
4. Laufer, p. 13.
5. Karlbeck, pp. 153–54.
6. Karlbeck, p. 176.
7. The quotations are from Laufer, p. 120, based upon E. Biot, *Le Tcheou-li*, 2 vols. (Paris 1851).
8. Willetts, 1:94.
9. Laufer, pp. 137–38.

10. Laufer, p. 37. The idea would appear to have remained current for many centuries after having been propounded by Liu Ngan. See Rudyard Kipling, *The Village That Voted the Earth Was Flat,* a short story published in 1913 and later collected in *A Diversity of Creatures.*

11. Hansford (1950), p. 100.

12. Hansford (1968), pp. 102–3 and plate 27.

13. Laufer, p. 197 and fig. 95.

14. Laufer, p. 327.

15. le Compte, p. 123.

16. See Fitzgerald, p. 554 ff. For eighteenth-century Canton see *Memoirs of William Hickey,* edited by A. Spencer, 4 vols. (1913–25), 1:194 ff.

17. Laufer, p. 247.

18. Hansford (1950), pp. 31–35.

19. Hansford (1950), pp. 5–12.

20. Watson (1962), p. 16.

21. Willetts, 1:19 and 1:108–9.

22. Karlbeck, p. 192.

23. See White.

24. Sullivan, 23:16–26.

25. Illustrated in Hansford (1968), plate 58.

26. Illustrated in Nott, plate 22.

27. Williams.

28. See Nott, plate 56, and Wills, plate 5.

29. Palmer, p. 41 and plate 20.

30. Williams, p. 131, and Nott, p. 72.

31. Laufer, p. 159.

CHAPTER 3

1. Bushell, 1:108, and David, p. vii.

2. Hansford (1968), p. 91 and plates 81a–b.

3. Hansford (1968), plate 83.

4. The T. B. Kitson Collection, Sotheby & Co., London (1960–61), lots 146 and 446.

5. Fitzgerald, pp. 548–49.

6. *Ching-tê Chên T'ao-lu,* p. 49.

7. Watson (1963).
8. Hansford (1950), pp. 74–78 and plate 27a.
9. Quoted in Watson, p. 33, from a translation by Dr. J. L. Mish.

CHAPTER 4

1. Pinder-Wilson, p. 19.
2. Wessels, p. 25.
3. Semedo, p. 18.
4. Lane, plate 70a.
5. The cups, now in the Archaeological Museum of Teheran, are illustrated in Hansford (1968), plates 80a–b.
6. Foster, pp. 102, 103.
7. Skelton.
8. Evans, p. 134, plates 114, figs. 23–24.
9. A marked Wan-li period (1573–1619) bowl inlaid with rubies and emeralds, in the Topkapi Palace Museum, Iznik, is illustrated in *Apollo,* vol. 92, no. 101 (July, 1970), p. 57, fig. 10.

CHAPTER 5

1. Hansford (1968), p. 30.
2. Illustrated in the Victoria and Albert Museum catalogue, but a better view of the crown, together with a close-up of the *magatama,* is given in Hansford (1968), plate 73.

CHAPTER 6

1. Harris, 1:326–27.
2. Cameron, p. 29.
3. Hansford (1950), p. 90.
4. *Gentleman's Magazine,* January, 1774, 44:20–21.
5. Read, p. 60.
6. Ruff, p. 64.

BIBLIOGRAPHY

[Barrow, John.] *Dictionarium Polygraphicum*. 2 vols. London: C. Hitch, C. Davis & S. Austen, 1735.

Burton, W. *Porcelain*. London & New York: Cassell, 1906.

Bushell, S. W. *Chinese Art*. 2 vols. 2nd ed. London: Victoria & Albert Museum, 1909 & 1910.

Cameron, H. C. *Sir Joseph Banks*. London: Batchworth, 1952.

Chhibber, H. L. *The Mineral Resources of Burma*. London: Macmillan, 1934.

Ching-tê Chên T'ao-lu. Trans. by G. R. Sayer. London: Faber & Faber, 1951.

David, Lady. *Illustrated Catalogue of Ch'ing Enamelled Wares*. London: Percival David Foundation, 1958.

Evans, Joan. *A History of Jewellery, 1100–1870*. 2nd ed. London: Faber & Faber, 1970.

Fitzgerald, C. P. *China: A Short Cultural History*. 2nd ed. London: Cresset Press, 1961.

Foster, W. *Early Travels in India*. Oxford: Oxford University Press, 1921.

Griffith, W. *Journal of Travels in Assam, Burma, etc.* Calcutta: 1847.

Hansford, S. Howard. *Chinese Carved Jade*. London: Faber & Faber, 1968.

——. *Chinese Jade Carving*. London: Lund Humphries, 1950.

Harris, John. *A Complete Collection of Voyages and Travels*. 2 vols. London: T. Woodward et al., 1744 and 1748.

Hertz, W. A. *Burma Gazetteer, Myitkyina District*. Volume A. Rangoon: 1912.

Karlbeck, Orvar. *Treasure Seeker in China*. London: Cresset Press, 1957.

Lane, Arthur. *Early Islamic Pottery*. London: Faber, 1947.

Laufer, Berthold. *Jade: A Study in Chinese Archaeology and Religion*. Vol. X. 1912. Reprint. New York: Kraus Reprint Co., 1967.

le Compte, Louis. *Memoirs and Observations . . . Made in a Late Journey Through the Empire of China*. London: B. Tooke & S. Buckley, 1697.

Nott, S. C. *Chinese Jade Throughout the Ages*. 1936. Reprint. Tokyo: Tuttle, 1962.

Palmer, J. P. *Jade*. London: Spring Books, 1967.

Pinder-Wilson, R., and Watson, W. "An Inscribed Jade Cup from Samarqand." *British Museum Quarterly*, vol. 23, no. 1 (September, 1930).

Read, A. W. *An Illustrated Encyclopedia of Maori Life*. Wellington: Read, 1950.

Ruff, Elsie. *Jade of the Maori*. London: Gemmological Association of Great Britain, 1950.

Scott, J. G., and Hardiman, J. P. *Gazetteer of Upper Burma and the Shan States.* 5 vols. Rangoon: 1900.

Semedo, Alvarez de. *The History of the Great and Renowned Monarchy of China.* Trans. by "a Person of quality." London: John Cook, 1655.

Skelton, Robert. "The Shah Jahan Cup." *Victoria and Albert Museum Bulletin,* vol. 2, no. 3 (July, 1966; reprinted, 1969).

Sullivan, Michael. "Excavations of the Royal Tomb of Wang Chien." *Transactions of the Oriental Ceramic Society,* vol. 23 (1947–48).

Victoria and Albert Museum. Catalogue of the exhibition of *National Art Treasures of Korea.* London: 1961.

Watson, W. *Ancient Chinese Bronzes.* London: Faber & Faber, 1962.

——. *Chinese Jade Books in the Chester Beatty Library.* Dublin: Hodges & Figgis, 1963.

Wessels, C. *Early Jesuit Travellers in Central Asia.* The Hague: Luzac, 1924.

White, W. C. *Tombs of Old Lo-yang.* Shanghai: 1934.

Willetts, William. *Chinese Art.* 2 vols. Harmondsworth: Penguin Books, 1958.

Williams, C. A. S. *Encyclopedia of Chinese Symbolism and Art Motives.* New York: Julian Press, 1960.

Wills, G. *Jade.* London: Arco, 1964.

Yule, Captain (later Sir) Henry. *Narrative of Major Phayre's Mission to the Court of Ava.* 1858. Reprinted in Oxford in Asia Reprints, Kuala Lumpur, 1968.

INDEX

This book is a joint production of John Weatherhill, Inc., of New York and Tokyo, and Orientations Ltd., of Hong Kong. Book design, typography, and layout by Dana Levy. Composition and printing of text by General Printing Company, Yokohama. Plates engraved and printed (in 5-color offset and monochrome gravure) by Nissha Printing Company, Kyoto. Bound at the Makoto Binderies, Tokyo. The typeface used throughout is Perpetua.